1

Introduction

TRYING TO understand a thinker of a past age is a task with two sides, between which it is essential to keep a proper balance. On the one side, we have to see him in the setting of the general conditions of his own age and place, and the special conditions of his own life. On the other, we have to be able to think his thought over again in our own minds. And, while we must always avoid the tendency to force him into the mould of contemporary theories, that does involve some degree of re-statement of his thought in terms of our own experience. It is with this latter side of the task that the present work is primarily concerned, and much of the essential knowledge of the history and conditions of the Greek world in Plato's age will have to be taken for granted. Even with regard to Plato's own life a good many details will have to be left to the reader to find out for himself. It is, however, desirable to recall certain of the main facts which are of particular importance for an understanding of his thought.

Plato was born in or about 427 B.C., the youngest son of an ancient and probably wealthy Athenian family. We know little of his early life. Aristotle tells us that in his youth he studied for a time under Cratylus, the disciple of Heraclitus, and there is every reason for supposing that his friendship with Socrates dated back to his early years. For the last five years of the Peloponnesian War he must have been engaged in military service. He tells us himself in one of his letters that his early ambitions were political, and after the end of the war he twice made the

attempt to enter on a political career, at first under the so-called
Thirty Tyrants, though their misdeeds speedily alienated him,
and again under the restored democracy, to whose moderation
he pays tribute in the letter just quoted. But from the democracy, too, he was alienated by the trial and execution of
Socrates in 399, and he never again attempted to participate
directly in Athenian politics. The first dozen years of the fourth
century were spent by him partly in travel abroad, culminating
in his first visit to the Greek cities in Italy and Sicily, when he
was about forty. But part of the time must again have been
spent in military service after the renewed outbreak of war. He
is said by later writers to have been decorated for valour on the
field in these campaigns. And this period must also have been
the start of his literary activity, with the production of the
earliest of the long series of dialogues which he gave to the
public throughout his life.

At some unspecified time after his return from Sicily, he
initiated what was to be the chief work of his life, with the foundation of the school or college known as the Academy. He pre-
sided over this till his death forty years or so later, and the
institution itself lived on for a continuous period of nine
hundred years, a longer span of life than any other educational
institution has yet known. It is reasonably certain that Plato's
primary object in founding the Academy was the training of
potential statesmen. He had come to the conclusion, as he tells
us in his letters, that there was no opening for a man of his standards in direct political activity of that time, but, as he again
tells us, he did not abandon hope of finding some way of making things better. The foundation of the Academy showed the
direction in which his hopes turned. It is clear that he hoped
by the training there to build up a group of men who would
approach political work in the spirit in which he thought it
should be approached, and that he hoped further that when
such men were produced the people in the Greek cities would
gradually come to have confidence in them and turn to them
for political leadership. Our information on the matter is very
scanty, but it is quite enough to show that he attained a considerable degree of success in his aim. His former pupils came
to play a leading part in many cities of Greece, and there seems

G. C. FIELD

The Philosophy of Plato

Second edition
with an Appendix by R. C. CROSS

OXFORD UNIVERSITY PRESS
Oxford London New York

Oxford University Press, Walton Street, Oxford OX2 6DP

OXFORD LONDON GLASGOW
NEW YORK TORONTO MELBOURNE WELLINGTON
IBADAN NAIROBI DAR ES SALAAM LUSAKA CAPE TOWN
KUALA LUMPUR SINGAPORE JAKARTA HONG KONG TOKYO
DELHI BOMBAY CALCUTTA MADRAS KARACHI

ISBN 0 19 888018 9

First published in the Home University Library *1949*
Second edition first published as an
Oxford University Press paperback 1969
Reprinted 1978

The General Editors of OPUS are
Keith Thomas (Humanities) and
J. S. Weiner (Sciences)

Used edition for
essay in 1978.

Printed in Great Britain
at the University Press, Oxford
by Vivian Ridler
Printer to the University

Contents

to have been a frequent tendency to call them in as experts in matters of legislation. We have a letter written by Plato to a former student who had been entrusted with the task of drawing up a code of laws for a new settlement and had written to the Academy for advice and help. Other students, however, turned their interests in a different direction. As any reader of the *Republic* would expect, the basis of the training was in scientific and philosophical studies, and some members came to devote themselves to these rather than to practical activities. The fourth century was a period of rapid scientific advance, particularly in mathematics and astronomy, and most of the progress in these subjects was due to the work of members of the Academy.

We know of two interruptions in Plato's career as a teacher. In 367 and again in 362 he went to Syracuse on the chance that it might be possible to convert the younger Dionysius, who had succeeded to his father's rule over the city in the former year, to the true philosophical principles of government. We are much more fully informed about these visits than about any other episode in Plato's life, largely through his own account in his letters, and the story is full of interest. But its importance as throwing light on Plato's character and outlook has often been exaggerated. The enterprise was not an adventure conceived by him on his own initiative. On the contrary, he only went to Syracuse very reluctantly under strong pressure from his friends and with very little hope of a successful outcome. His pessimism was well founded, and for a variety of causes both attempts failed. Into the further tangled story of Syracusan politics we need not enter. Plato kept up his interest in them to some degree, but made no further attempt at personal intervention. He died in 347 at the age of eighty.

This brief account will make it clear that the popular conception of Plato as an aloof unworldly scholar, spinning theories in his study remote from practical life, is singularly wide of the mark. On the contrary, he was a man of the world, an experienced soldier, widely travelled, with close contacts with many of the leading men of affairs, both in his own city and elsewhere. It will also confirm the impression that a discriminating reading of his dialogues should give that his central interest throughout his life was the practical one of the reform of society. That is not, however, incompatible with a love of knowledge for its own sake. He certainly held that those who were capable of philosophical thinking would find that the pursuit of truth was an occupation that, if they consulted only their own personal tastes, would be more completely satisfying than any other. But it was just for those people that the obligation was strongest to do what they could directly or indirectly for the betterment of their society. And this was an obligation that was clearly in Plato's mind in all his work.

A fresh problem arises when we consider the material that we have for our knowledge of Plato's philosophical views. There is no systematic treatise, such as we are accustomed to with other philosophers, in which these views are set out. Apart from some references in Aristotle, which in any case only refer to Plato's later years, we are dependent upon the dialogues, of which we have some thirty, the great majority certainly genuine though a few are doubtful. These are a series of conversation pieces, and, in interpreting them, there are several points to be borne in mind. For one thing, we must remember that, beside being the vehicles of profound thought, they are also, with very few exceptions, supreme expressions of Plato's literary and dramatic genius. They show the mastery of language, the power of indicating character, the sense of a situation, and the keen eye for both its tragic and its comic aspects, which set Plato among the greatest writers of the world. He uses these gifts to the full in inculcating the lessons that he wants to teach. But we shall be safe in saying that, in all his writings, with one or two possible exceptions, it is the serious thought that is the aim, and the literary gifts are subordinated to that. None the less, the dramatic element is there and often has to be allowed for in the detailed interpretation of particular passages.

In the present work, however, we are not concerned, except incidentally, with the literary aspect, but with the philosophical ideas. And in trying to arrive at these, one or two difficulties of interpretation face us. One arises from the familiar fact that in all the dialogues, except a few of the latest, the principal part is taken by Socrates, and Plato never appears by name at all. This has given rise to a vigorous discussion in the past as to the degree to which the positive views set out or implied in the dialogues can be ascribed to the historical Socrates. We need not linger over this. To most scholars the evidence seems pretty clear that Socrates himself had no systematic positive doctrine to teach, but was rather a stimulating and critical influence. The positive doctrines in the dialogues, so far as there are any, are Plato's own. At any rate, it is clear that for practical purposes they must be regarded as such. To us the philosophy of Plato can only mean the philosophy expressed or implied in the Platonic dialogues. For we know no other.

A much more difficult critical question arises when we consider the way in which we can use these dialogues to reconstruct Plato's views. He makes quite definite statements more than once in his letters to the effect that his fundamental philosophical position could not possibly be set out in a formal written treatise. It could only be understood when we came to see it for ourselves after prolonged thought and questioning and discussion. Even allowing for a certain amount of exaggeration in this, due to the circumstances in which the letters were written, we have to take such a statement seriously. It does not mean that we cannot find out anything about Plato's fundamental ideas. But it does mean that we cannot find them ready-made for us in the dialogues. The dialogues are really a series of occasional essays, cast in the form of conversations, on particular questions which were of interest sometimes to the general public and sometimes to the narrower circle of those with a special bent for philosophy. The general points of view from which these questions are approached are very often implied rather than stated, and, when stated, very rarely argued at length. Further, Plato, who evidently took his writings less seriously as an expression of his opinions than we have to do, in all probability allowed himself the latitude, appropriate to a conversation, of thinking aloud and from time to time putting forward tentatively and experimentally ideas to which he would not have wished to be finally committed. There is always, therefore, a certain sense of adventure in coming to a conclusion about Plato's settled views and some differences of opinion will always be possible. None the less the attempt is well worth making, and on some of the most important points it is possible to arrive at conclusions which would be fairly generally accepted by those who have given the most careful study to Plato's works.

One more point may be mentioned in passing. These discussions of particular questions, particularly in the later dialogues, clearly imply a general philosophical position from which they are approached. We need not suppose that Plato had ever arrived at a complete and final philosophical system that left no questions unanswered. But he was obviously, like every serious philosopher, aiming at this and trying to make his thought as systematic as possible. He does not, however, first arrive at his general view and then deduce from it automatically the solution of all these particular problems. He approaches each particular problem afresh and a great deal of what he has to say about it can be understood and argued without reference to his general view. This adds greatly to the interest of the dialogues. But it also adds to the difficulty of selection for anyone who tries to give an account of Plato's views in a relatively small compass. There will always, therefore, be the possibility of difference of opinion about the best selection as well as about the interpretation of the views, and it is quite likely that some readers, who would accept my account as accurate as far as it goes, would still complain that I had omitted some of the most interesting points. That, however, is inevitable.

If we use the indications that he has given us it is not difficult to imagine the state of mind in which Plato began his literary work. The execution of Socrates clearly came as a tremendous shock to him. To understand what a shock it was, we have to try to picture to ourselves what Socrates meant to him. Historians of Philosophy tend, naturally enough, to stress particularly the intellectual influence of Socrates, the stimulus that he gave to thought by his untiring readiness to question and discuss and by the skill that he showed in the use of the method of argument by question and answer, which is pictured to us in his early dialogues. That is important, but it would not have accounted for Socrates' peculiar influence if it had not been combined with an unflinching moral rectitude and courage to pursue without swerving the course that he thought was right. It is as his ideal of the righteous man that Socrates made his appeal to Plato above all else. We must remember that Plato grew up in a period of a widespread breakdown of accepted moral standards. Prolonged war and intensified civil strife throughout Greece had done much to bring this about. But alongside of that there went the development, which had already begun a generation earlier, of certain speculative views in the direction of scepticism both about the possibility of attaining the truth and about the validity of any moral standards at all. There were plenty who argued that all moral restraints were merely artificial man-made conventions, and that the enlightened man who saw through these would merely use them to bamboozle other people, but for himself would pursue without scruple his selfish personal desires. Plato gives us in the *Gorgias* a vivid picture of the type of ruthless political adventurer who used these sceptical arguments to justify his own lack of scruple.

To young men of keen and active intelligence and of generous spirit it must have been a bewildering time. They could not, as many of their elders would have recommended, cease to think and return to the uncritical acceptance of conventional standards. On the other hand, they could not reconcile themselves, as so many of their contemporaries did, to the abandonment of all standards. We can well imagine that, to many of those who knew him, the figure of Socrates must have appeared as something in the nature of a sheet-anchor in the shifting tides of the time. For here was a man who was quite ready to meet the critics and the sceptics on their own ground and to carry questioning and discussion as far as they would go, and who yet never lost faith that there was a truth which it was worth while seeking and that there was a right and wrong which it was worth while pursuing or avoiding in our own lives. He may never have attained to a positive theoretical doctrine which he could give them, but he gave them the example of his own life and few who knew him were untouched by it. It is small wonder, then, that his death should have such a decisive effect on the attitude of a man like Plato towards the society which was responsible for it.

It is a reasonable conclusion, then, that the purpose of the earlier dialogues was to carry on the work of Socrates by stimulating thought through the methods of discussion that he had used at the same time—for the two are not really separate aims —to defend his memory and justify his services to the world. It is customary to speak of these earlier dialogues as Socratic dialogues in the strictest sense, and it is probable that the general picture of Socrates and his methods is substantially true to life. But they are certainly nothing in the nature of verbatim reports, the choice of subject and the actual presentation are Plato's, and from the beginning it is Plato's thought which is presented, even if it runs very much on the lines suggested to him by Socrates. It would be perfectly natural, therefore, that as Plato went on writing he should put more and more of the ideas that he had arrived at for himself into his work, until he had gone much beyond anything that Socrates ever thought of. It does not much matter for our present purposes at what stage that begins, though most scholars feel pretty confident about some of the most important points. But that is a matter of more interest for a discussion of Socrates' thought than of Plato's.

What, then, were the chief contributions made in these earlier dialogues? Later commentators, from Aristotle onwards, have tended to single out for attention the importance of the search for precise definitions of the terms under discussion. This is a marked feature of many of these dialogues, and is applied particularly to general terms used in the discussion of questions of conduct. Courage, piety, self-control, friendship—each of these in turn is the special subject of a particular dialogue. There is no need to stress the value for clear thinking of a demand for precise definitions of the general terms used, and there is little doubt that Socrates and Plato after him were among the first to realize the importance of this. The familiar move in a discussion, 'It depends what you mean by' so-and-so, may really be said to be the invention of Socrates.

But there is more in it than that. It is significant that in these early dialogues the speakers never do arrive at a finally acceptable definition, and their difficulty is nearly always the same. It arises from the fact that they set out to define a particular virtue or moral quality in a way which will distinguish it from other virtues. And then, as they go along, they find themselves obliged to speak of it in terms which seem to make it identical with the whole of virtue. Thus, if we assume courage to be a virtue, and then define it, say, as disregard of danger, we see on reflection that there are occasions on which it would be wrong to disregard danger. It cannot be a virtue to do what is wrong, and therefore courage cannot consist in this, but rather in disregarding danger when it is right or good to do so, and not when it is wrong or evil. But that cannot be done without a knowledge and understanding of what is good and what is evil. To put it another way, there may be all sorts of tendencies to act in this or that way, in this particular case to disregard danger. But what makes the tendency a virtue, in this case courage, is the knowledge of good and evil which controls it. And just the same can be said of other virtues, so that the essential feature of all of them is the same. This is a very bald and inadequate summary of the kind of argument that recurs in a number of these early dialogues.

It will be seen that the central point that emerges in them is that the essential feature that makes any virtue a virtue is knowledge of what is good and what bad. And it is often said that Socrates, and Plato in these earlier dialogues, identify virtue and knowledge. But that is only partially true. All that the argument requires is that knowledge is the one essential feature of any virtue, not necessarily that it is the whole of it. And, in any case, it is evident that Plato is not completely satisfied with this, and refrains from drawing any final conclusion. But what is more important to note is that so far as the equation of virtue and knowledge is accepted it is not a private invention of Socrates or Plato but arises naturally from the development of ordinary Greek moral assumptions. For the word which we translate 'good' ($\dot{\alpha}\gamma\alpha\theta\acute{o}s$), which is the chief Greek moral category, in itself would suggest to any Greek some connexion with what is wanted or desired or aimed at. Naturally, of course, he would realize that many things that were in fact desired by particular people at particular times were far from being what he would call good. But it is not too much to say that it would have seemed to him a contradiction in terms to call anything good if it had no connexion with what, in some sense or under some conditions, would be desired by or would satisfy people. Starting from such an assumption that good implied somehow in some sense what was wanted, it was very natural to go on to the further assumption that at any rate the primary, if not the sole and sufficient, condition for attaining it was to know what it was and what would produce it.

It is the same with the word ἀρετή (*aretē*), which we generally translate as 'virtue', though in some contexts 'goodness' might be a better rendering. It is, I think, fair to say that when, in current English, we use the terms 'virtue' or 'virtuous' the first unthinking suggestion that comes to our minds is the negative one of the avoidance of the various kinds of wrong-doing. No doubt on further reflection we should not be satisfied with this, but that would be our first reaction to the word. For the Greek it would be different. Doubtless he would use the corresponding term in much the same connexions as we should. Courage, self-control, justice would be called virtues by us and ἀρεταί by him. But in so calling them the first suggestion that would be conveyed to his mind would be of some sort of positive ability or capacity for doing something. Thus, at the beginning of the *Republic* when the discussion is still at the level of ordinary conversation, Socrates can speak quite naturally and casually of justice or righteousness as an art or acquired skill. We might come to talk of it like that ourselves, but it would need a good deal of reflection and explanation before it could be accepted as a natural way of speaking. The discussion that follows in the dialogue shows that we get into serious confusion if we think of it merely as one special kind of skill alongside others. But the general notion of moral goodness as, in some sense, an art or skill, as knowing how to do something, remains, and is simply the development of ordinary Greek moral assumptions. Nor is it so very difficult for us, on reflection, to accept this as a description of, at any rate, one aspect of right conduct.

But if we thus come to think of moral goodness as in some sense knowing how to do something, it is only natural to suppose that it ought to be capable of being taught. And this question of the possibility of moral education occupies the attention of the speakers in these earlier dialogues even more, perhaps, than the search for definitions. Indeed, in some of them the search for definitions seems, at times, to be pursued simply as a means towards deciding the best methods of inculcating the moral qualities discussed. But the discussions on this point appear even further from reaching positive results. It does not appear possible to find any recognized and authoritative teachers, nor any generally accepted conclusions to be taught. There is a sharp contrast to be drawn here with the exact sciences and the technical crafts. And Plato evidently, like many modern thinkers, is strongly impressed by the relative clearness and certainty of our conclusions in these latter fields as compared with the uncertainties and disagreements which mark our thinking about human conduct.

In one or two of the early dialogues, for instance in the *Protagoras* and to some extent in the *Meno*, the suggestion is put into the mouths of some of the speakers that all the knowledge that we wanted on this was given us by the accepted rules of right conduct which were embodied in the laws and conventions of our society, and that the instruction necessary in this was contained in what we learned as we grew up from the people around us. But this attitude clearly would not do. It had broken down in practice, and it was theoretically helpless in face of the sceptical criticisms to which we have already referred. Against such criticisms even the most admirable conventional code could not maintain itself as long as it remained merely conventional and could not give a reasoned account and defence of itself. It was easy to point out that the accepted conventions differed widely from one society to another, and in all ages it has seemed to many that the natural conclusion to be drawn from that was that they had no basis in reality and no objective validity at all. They could, therefore, have no claim on any individuals who had once seen through them.

This sceptical view, if we can judge by the indications that Plato gives us, took various forms. The negative criticism was much the same in all. But they seem to have varied somewhat in the accounts they gave of how the idea of morality ever came to exist at all if it had no basis in reality. One of the most drastic explanations is that put into the mouth of Thrasymachus, in the *Republic*. According to that, the standards of morality in any society were simply the expression of the selfish personal interests of the particular individuals or groups which dominated that society, and were imposed by force or fraud on the rest. Other less extreme theories were put forward. But they all had this in common, that morality and the restraints it involved had no basis in the nature of human beings or of reality as a whole, and that the sensible man would naturally disregard them whenever he could do so safely and conveniently.

Typical presentations of this view are criticized by Plato, rather inadequately in the First Book of the *Republic* and much more thoroughly and convincingly in the *Gorgias*. But these are *ad hoc* criticisms of particular presentations of it, and do not attempt to provide a positive basis for an alternative view. It was not enough to show that particular sceptics contradicted themselves. If the validity of moral judgements was to be established against any possible objections, it would need a much more searching inquiry into their ultimate status and origin. And that was the challenge that Plato was to take up in his later writings.

But before going on to that, a further word must be said to make clear Plato's attitude to sceptical criticism of accepted codes and conventions. He himself was far from thinking that it was possible or desirable to go back to an uncritical acceptance of the conventional standards of every society, and he was a severe critic of much of the conventional morality of his own time and place. The standards of the society which condemned Socrates, for instance, could hardly be accepted as they stood. But that does not mean that we can get rid of conventions altogether. Everyone is bound to take over a large part of the actual content of his moral code from the accepted standards of the society in which he lives. An independent moral thinker may criticize and even defy this moral code in particular points, but, even in his revolt, he never frees himself from its influence altogether and over a large field its claim on him will remain unquestioned. In that beautiful little dialogue, the *Crito*, Plato shows how even the great non-conformist Socrates recognized and accepted this. It is really a vain illusion to suppose that everyone all the time ever does or ever could decide what is right and wrong entirely by himself by the unaided exercise of his personal judgement. The sceptical critic is therefore right in supposing that in practice there must necessarily be a considerable conventional element in moral conduct. Where he is wrong is in supposing that that necessarily deprives it of all claim on us.

There is a further point of importance. Even the cynical analysis by Thrasymachus of the way in which the moral codes of societies become established is not entirely devoid of truth. Indeed, as an account of some actual societies, Plato would certainly have felt that there was only too much truth in it, even if it was never the whole truth. But it does call attention to the undeniable fact that in building up and establishing the accepted code of any society some people in that society will inevitably have much more influence than others. Further, which those people are to be will be determined to a great extent by the structure and organization of that particular society. It follows, then, that the question of the proper organization of society— i.e. politics in the widest sense—is inseparably bound up with morality, the establishment of a code of right conduct for individuals. For most of us all the time and for all of us most of the time it is the society in which we live that sets our moral standards. What those moral standards are will be largely determined by the way in which that society is organized, and conversely the way in which we think the society ought to be organized will be largely determined by the moral standards that we think it ought to set. We cannot think about the one without also thinking about the other.

It would not, I think, be seriously disputed that that was the general standpoint from which Plato approached the further examination of these questions. And it is hardly less certain that it was the standpoint that any Greek thinker of his time would naturally tend to adopt. Today, also, anyone who thought on these matters would have to recognize that there was a very great deal of truth in it. It would be out of place to attempt to discuss in detail exactly how far we could accept it as it stands. But it is necessary, in order to enable us to understand Plato, to indicate certain differences between our own time and his which would make us express the point in rather different terms, even though a fundamental identity remained.

One point that often perplexes the student in his first reading of Plato and other Greek writers is the frequent reference to the law as the chief expression of the standards of right and wrong. It is undoubtedly true that the ordinary Greek tended to look to the law to tell him what his moral duties were much more readily than we should. He expected legislation to deal with matters that we should not think appropriate for it at all, and he expected the law courts to enforce what we should think of as purely moral judgements and not to confine themselves to the application of explicit legislative enactments. The oft-quoted remark of English judges, 'This is not a court of morals', would have been unintelligible to the ordinary Athenian juryman. This does not necessarily mean that we are any more ready than the Greeks to use our individual judgement and consider each case afresh on its own merits. It does mean that, where they looked to positive law enforceable in the courts to tell them what ought or ought not to be done, we look more naturally to conventional codes of conduct enforceable only by public opinion. This is not an absolute distinction. The Greek did not suppose that every moral question could be decided by the law, and we do not suppose that the law has nothing to do with morality. But there is a considerable difference of emphasis, and we shall often best get the point of discussions about the nature and authority of law in Plato and other Greek writers if we try applying them with the necessary modifications to the conventional codes of morality in a modern society.

For another thing, the political unit in which the Greek lived was the city-state, a small concentrated community, very close to all the individuals in it, in which the lesser societies within it, though not entirely unimportant, played very minor parts. In a larger, more diffuse community such as ours, the smaller societies within it—the locality, the church, the political party, the professional organization, and all the rest—play a much greater part in the lives of the individuals who belong to them, and we look to them for a great deal for which the Greek would naturally turn to his city. It is, for instance, one of the commonest illusions in our own day for people to think that they have freed themselves from the shackles of convention because they set themselves against certain conventions current throughout the wider society of their nation, whereas in fact they are following rigidly the conventions of some smaller group to which they belong. Again, the performance of his public duties to the city, particularly in a democracy such as Athens, filled a much greater place in the life of the individual than it would for the great majority in our own country. That, however, is a difference of degree, not of kind, and did not rule out the recognition of his duties towards his individual neighbours and the smaller societies to which he belonged.

To return to the main argument, we can now begin to see the way in which the problem was formulating itself in Plato's mind in these earlier years. The challenge he had to meet was twofold. There was on the one side the challenge of the sceptical philosophies, adopted in practice by many who had but the vaguest knowledge of the theories, which cast doubts on the possibility of there being any objective validity, any basis in the nature of reality, for moral judgements at all. On the other there was the challenge of the facts of the situation, which revealed the absence of any established and agreed body of knowledge on the problems of conduct at all comparable to the established body of scientific knowledge which already existed. Was it possible to find an objective criterion of right and wrong which could be known with the certainty of scientific knowledge, and could form a basis for the moral judgements of the individual, for the criticism of existing moral codes, and for the eventual establishment of the true moral code of a reformed society?

We may pause here to reflect for a moment on the kind of answer that we can legitimately expect to such questions. Strictly speaking, the challenge to establish the validity of moral judgements against any possible objection can never be met. The sceptic, if he is determined enough, the 'single resolute doubter' to whom appeal is sometimes made, can never be finally answered, because he can always demand further proof of the validity of any argument that is offered him, and if he persists in saying that he cannot see it there is nothing more to be done. This applies to any kind of knowledge, scientific as much as moral, and there were sceptics in Plato's time and later who challenged the validity of scientific or indeed any kind of reasoning. We have references to them in some of the dialogues, though we do not get the impression that they were taken so seriously as those who raised doubts about the validity of moral judgements. But with regard to these latter it should be obvious that we cannot possibly, as sometimes appears to be demanded, prove that there is such a thing as morality by deduction from something else which is not morality. We can only start with the fact of moral judgements, and try to discover what is implied or assumed in them about the kind of thinking which is valid and the nature of the reality about which we think. We can show that possible objections are not decisive and that apparent contradictions can be avoided. And we can work this up into a coherent and systematic account, consistent with itself and with the rest of our knowledge. But in the final resort each one has to make the decision for himself whether he can accept this or not.

If we want to do this we cannot confine our considerations to moral judgements alone. To show that moral judgements have at any rate as much validity as any other kind of judgement, we must examine the general nature and conditions of valid thinking, particularly in scientific thought, which to a Greek of Plato's time would naturally be taken to be most completely exemplified in mathematics. But this leads us further. By correct thinking we imply thinking that gives us knowledge about reality, about the real facts or what really is the case as opposed to what only appears to be so. And to answer the question whether any particular kind of thinking gives us knowledge about reality we must ask what we mean by reality, what our test or criterion of the real is. So, perplexities about the possibility of moral judgements lead on inevitably to an attempt to work out a general theory of the nature of reality, and this is what we mean by Metaphysics. It is to Plato's metaphysical theory, then, that we must now turn.

2
The Theory of Forms (1)

IN HIS metaphysical theory, Plato is attempting to answer the question, *What is real?* This is not, as some modern writers have seemed to suggest, a question invented by philosophers for their own amusement. On the contrary, it arises inevitably as soon as we begin to reflect on our most ordinary thought and experience. All our thinking and investigation from the first is an attempt to find out what is real or what really is the case, as opposed to what only appears to be. This distinction between reality and appearance is, therefore, assumed in our ordinary experience from its earliest stages, and any constructive thinker has to give some account of it. The modern philosopher has been enabled, perhaps not always to his advantage, to introduce many subtleties into his discussion of the problem by the variety of terms at his disposal in our own language. He can speak of what is, of what exists, of what is real, and, if he adopts the suggestion of a distinguished modern scientist, of what is 'really real'. Plato had not our opportunities, since classical Greek only gave him the different parts of the verb 'to be', though he does on occasion speak of 'that which truly is' (τὸ ἀληθῶς ὄν). But the question is essentially the same in whatever language we express it.

Now, the first point to notice in Plato's answer to the question is his uncompromising denial of reality to what we ordinarily call the real world, the objects which we see and touch and hear around us in our everyday life. For him the objects which we perceive by our senses are not real. To the plain man this may seem at first sight highly paradoxical, and some modern critics of Plato have been so shocked by it that they have looked for all sorts of discreditable explanations. Some contemporary writers denounce him as a reactionary aristocrat with a snobbish contempt for the workaday world. A generation or so ago it was more fashionable to talk of him as a visionary dreamer anxious to escape from solid reality into a supersensible world of his own. But all this way of talking is very ill-judged. In reality he had thoroughly hard-headed reasons for his views, whether we agree with them or not. As we shall see in a moment, they are merely an extension of ways of thinking which are quite familiar to ordinary common sense. And further, they are no special peculiarity of Plato's but were shared, in some form or to some degree, by nearly all the thinkers of his own age or earlier.

It is, of course, an elementary fact of experience that, at the ordinary common-sense level, though we say readily enough that what we see, touch, etc., is the real world, in practice we unhesitatingly reject probably as much as ninety per cent of what we perceive by our senses as not being real at all. What we perceive by our senses consists of various qualities, colour, shape, heat and cold, and the like, which we ordinarily ascribe to certain objects. But the qualities that we actually perceive vary indefinitely with a variety of conditions, and so far as they depend on these conditions we say that they are not real. Thus they vary with the state of our sense-organs, like the colours seen by a colour-blind man or the shapes seen by a person suffering from astigmatism. They vary with the position relative to us, like all the different shapes of an object we see from different angles. They vary with variations in external conditions, as when a straight stick looks bent when seen through water, or the colours that we see change with every change of light. So far as it depends on these things, we say normally that it is not the real shape or the real colour that we see, and the same applies, of course, *mutatis mutandis* to the qualities perceived by the other senses. We see on reflection, therefore, that we are quite familiar with the idea that we perceive a great deal by our senses that we do not regard as real. Indeed, we ordinarily suppose that we only perceive the real quality under certain standard conditions that are comparatively rarely attained. I do not think, for instance, that I have ever actually seen what I suppose to be the real shape of the surface of my table.

In these cases common sense assumes that there is a real object with a real shape, colour, etc., though we very rarely perceive it as it really is. But in other cases we go further still. For in dreams and hallucinations we have an experience of perceiving things which is entirely indistinguishable, as far as the experience goes, from perceiving what we call real objects. Yet we dismiss unhesitatingly everything that we perceive under these conditions as having no reality in it at all. It is interesting to note that Plato, in one of his later dialogues, suggests as a possible starting-point for philosophical reflection that we should put the question to ourselves how we can ever know that we are not dreaming.

We need, therefore, very little reflection to see that we certainly do not in practice regard the fact that we perceive something by our senses as any proof of its reality. But in accepting some and rejecting the rest of what we so perceive we must be acting on certain principles of selection, even though we never formulate them to ourselves and perhaps do not always apply them decisively and consistently. We must have in our mind, however vaguely and confusedly, certain conditions that must be fulfilled before anything can be accepted as real, or, in other words, certain assumptions about the general nature of reality.

It is the essence of assumptions of this kind that they are acted on rather than clearly conceived. So far as they are conceived it is only vaguely, so that there is always a risk of being misleading if we try to state them too precisely. But there are certain things that seem to appear fairly clearly. We should assume, for instance, that to be 'really there' the quality that we perceive must belong to its object independently of the condition of the person perceiving and, to some extent, of other surrounding conditions and circumstances. Connected with that is another demand that we seem to make, the demand for a certain degree of permanence and stability in what we are going to accept as real. We do not, of course, at the common-sense level suppose that to be real a thing must not change or decay at all.

But we do feel that it ought not to change too much or too readily, certainly not as readily as what we actually perceive by the senses does. For this, as we have seen, changes continuously with every change in our own position relatively to it, in the conditions of our sense-organs, and in the surrounding circumstances.

Another demand that we seem to make is for a certain standard of precision and definiteness in what is to be accepted as real. We assume, for instance, that the real quality of an object must belong to it exclusively of any other quality of the same kind. If a thing is 'really' red it cannot be some other colour at the same time, if it is 'really' square it cannot also be another shape. To put it in more general terms, we assume that a real object must be either this or that and not both at once. That means that what is really the case ought to be capable of being stated in clear and unequivocal assertions, which, if true at all, are completely true. And until we can do that we are not satisfied that we have discovered the reality.

It is by the application of some such conditions as these that we come in our ordinary experience to reject such a large proportion of what we perceive by our senses as not being real. But after we have made them explicit we may well begin to wonder whether a more consistent application of them would not result in the rejection of the small fraction that remained. After all, we never perceive anything except by means of sense-organs which must be in a certain condition, and we never perceive anything except from a certain position and in a context of surrounding circumstances. It certainly seems rather arbitrary to pick out one set of conditions as giving us the real facts, though there is nothing in the actual experience of perceiving to enable us to distinguish these conditions from those which give us what is not real. We may well ask ourselves whether a more consistent application of these tests would not force us to reject everything that was perceived by the senses at all.

To the plain man it might naturally appear as if something like this had happened in the development of that specially coherent and systematic kind of thinking that we call scientific. When we consider the results of this and survey the picture that modern physical science presents to us, we should certainly feel that it gave us a real world startlingly unlike anything that we perceive by the senses. It was bad enough when we were told that the objects that we saw as solid and continuous and motionless were really made up of countless whirling atoms. But when the atom gave place to the electron and other objects more mysterious still, the remoteness of the 'real' world of physics from the sensible world became more striking than ever. Some leaders of scientific thought have been so worried by this that they have become reluctant to use terms like 'real' and 'reality' at all. But the ordinary man still does, and, if he has a bowing acquaintance with the general results of modern physics, he still talks, as most scientists did till very recently, of the world of scientific theory as the real world. Or perhaps it would be more accurate to say that he believes both in a 'real world' which we can see and touch and a 'really real world' of physics which has no resemblance to the former.

It would be impossible here to survey the development of scientific thought in detail to see how it arrived at this result. But it is certainly a plausible suggestion that, in part at any rate, the result was due to the continuous application of some of the criteria of reality touched upon above.

One of these has certainly played a great part in the development of scientific thought, and that is the demand that the results of the scientist's search for reality should be capable of being expressed in precise and definite statements which are unequivocally true. This is the ideal which is always aimed at in all thinking, and if we assume that our thinking is directed towards the discovery of what is real, it follows that we are also assuming that what is real must be such that it can be expressed in this kind of statement. This idea has a long history. It was first definitely formulated in ancient Greece, most clearly by Parmenides, and it is basic to Plato's thought, who expressed it in the phrase 'the completely real is the completely intelligible' (παντελῶς ὄν, παντελῶς γνωστόν). But there was a special form that was given to it by other Greek thinkers, Pythagoras and his followers, and made use of in his own way by Plato. That is the idea that the reality which scientific thought is seeking must be expressible in mathematical terms, mathematics being the most precise and definite kind of thinking of which we are capable. The significance of this idea for the development of science from the first beginnings to the present day has been immense.

The other idea that has played a great part is the idea that what is completely real must be permanent. As we have already seen, even at the common-sense level we approach the idea tentatively, though we certainly do not accept it as it stands. But in the kind of thinking that has been responsible for the development of science it has been accepted much more definitely. Early Greek scientific thought was directed towards finding some substance which was always there and always remained the same under all apparent changes and differences of the physical world. And after the principle was definitely formulated, once more through the influence of Parmenides, it became the basis of almost all Greek scientific speculation. The actual results of this speculation are mostly of little interest to us now. But one of the forms it took was the famous atomic theory, and this was the lineal ancestor of modern theories of matter, greatly though they have modified the original form.

We can hardly attempt to trace the influence of this general idea throughout the history of scientific thought. But it can at least be said that it has played a great part as a guiding principle in scientific investigation down to modern times. It has been expressed in the various theories of conservation down to the law of the Conservation of Energy, which is its most recent form. A scientist of our own day, Professor Frederick Soddy, gave expression to the idea in the words which he wrote in his book *Matter and Energy* a quarter of a century ago. 'Gradually,' he says, 'this law of conservation has supplied the physicist with an experimental test of reality in a changing universe. What appears and disappears mysteriously, giving no clue to its origin or destination, is outside of his province. To him it has no physical existence. What is conserved has physical existence.' Or again, 'Deep down somewhere in the processes of thought the ultimate test of reality appears to be the law of Conservation.'

There are, no doubt, possible alternative explanations and interpretations of all this. But we are not concerned to defend the view against any possible criticism. All that is aimed at here is to show that it is a view that can reasonably be held. And it is sufficiently clear that, in adopting these criteria of reality, Plato was simply working along the same lines as many other thinkers, from his Greek predecessors down to the present day. And it is equally clear that if we adopt these criteria and apply them seriously we cannot accept the world perceived by the senses as 'really real'. It is in a state of continual change, instead of having the permanence and stability that we require, and, because of that and for other reasons too, it has not got the definite and determinate character that we demand of what is real. So we find that the rejection of the sensible world as not real is no special peculiarity of Plato's. It is a position that is shared, to some degree, by almost all the leading thinkers of ancient Greece. It is, for instance, expressed clearly by Democritus and the Atomists, who in other respects hold views sharply divergent from Plato's.

I have dwelt on this at length because of the truly extraordinary misunderstandings of Plato's position on this point which make their appearance so often, even among people who ought to know better. It is more important, however, to ask where Plato turned to find objects which would pass these tests of reality. Where does he look for facts which are 'really there' to be discovered, which are permanent and unaffected by the passage of time, and which have definite and determinate characteristics that make them possible objects of exact scientific knowledge?

It was only natural that he should turn in the first place to the most developed kind of scientific knowledge of his time, namely mathematics. It is a pure conjecture, but I am inclined to connect the original development of his theory with his first visit to Italy and Sicily at about the age of forty. For there, in all probability, he came into close contact with groups of Pythagoreans, particularly at Tarentum where Archytas was already coming into prominence as both a mathematician and a statesman, and it was among the Pythagoreans, until the centre of the subject moved to Plato's Academy, that mathematics was most systematically studied. Be that as it may, it was in the objects studied in mathematics that he seemed to find

the most obvious instances of the true realities that he was looking for.

Consider the most elementary instance possible of a mathematical proposition. When we say that $1 + 1 = 2$, we naturally
suppose that we are stating a fact which is there for us to discover: we certainly do not make it up. What we assert is true
permanently and independently of the passage of time, not true
at some times and false at others. It is true independently of the
surrounding circumstances. And it is absolutely and definitely
and unequivocally true, not approximately true or true from
some points of view and not from others. In other words, the
facts stated in this, or any other, mathematical proposition
seem to fulfil exactly the tests of reality that Plato adopted.

There are, of course, certain modern theories of the nature
of mathematics which would cast doubt on what they would
regard as this simple-minded view. Plato, naturally, was not
acquainted with modern theories. But even nowadays the practising mathematician seems naturally inclined to adopt a view
very like this. In a book by one of the most distinguished of
them, G. H. Hardy's *A Mathematician's Apology*, we read, 'It
seems to me that no philosophy can possibly be sympathetic
to a mathematician which does not admit, in one manner or
another, the immutable and unconditional validity of mathematical truth. . . . In *some* sense, mathematical truth is part of
objective reality. . . . These [theorems of which three examples
are given] . . . are, in one sense or another, however elusive that
sense may be, theorems concerning reality. . . . They are not
creations of our minds; Lagrange discovered the first in 1774;
when he discovered it, he discovered *something*; and to that
something Lagrange and the year 1774 are equally indifferent.'
There seems to me little or nothing here that Plato would have
found difficulty in accepting.

A further important point for Plato is that these mathematical propositions do not apply with the same absolute,
eternal, and unequivocal truth to sensible objects. To these they
seem to apply in a certain sense or to a certain degree, but not
absolutely and unconditionally. Even in simple arithmetic, for
instance, the proposition $1 + 1 = 2$ is only absolutely and unconditionally true if we take the 'one' to be one and nothing

else. But no sensible object is ever just one and nothing else. It is one only from certain points of view or it can be treated as one for certain purposes, but for others it is many, and it is not 'really' one any more than it is many. But perhaps for illustrating Plato's point we can find a clearer example if we turn to the propositions of geometry, which for the purpose of understanding Greek thought we must take as meaning Euclidean geometry.

Here we are presented with certain objects such as points, which are defined as having position but no magnitude, or lines which have length and no breadth, or surfaces which have length and breadth but no thickness, and we prove propositions about these things and about different figures made up of them. But we know that we cannot actually draw or make these things or observe them in the world around us. We can, for instance, get nearer and nearer to a line the finer we draw it, but in the nature of things we cannot either draw or observe a line with absolutely *no* breadth. That is a very simple instance, but the same thing applies to more complicated figures. We find something very like it also, in other branches of mathematics, where, for instance, we deal with absolutely rigid bodies or absolutely pure fluids, about which we can prove various propositions, but which we never have met and never will meet among the sensible objects around us.

Now, all these mathematical objects appear to be real by all the tests of reality suggested above. They are certainly something that we have to discover, and are not just invented or made up. And what we discover about them can be expressed in absolutely clear and unequivocal statements. We do not, however, discover them in the objects of sense-perception, which, as we have seen, never have completely the characteristics of mathematical objects. For that reason we cannot, as is sometimes supposed, arrive at their characteristics by a process of abstraction, i.e. leaving out or 'thinking away' the other qualities that we perceive in the sensible objects until we are left with one perceived quality in isolation. For the qualities of the mathematical objects are not found in the sensible objects at all. Similarly the propositions that we prove about the mathematical objects, e.g. the geometrical circle or square, never apply completely and absolutely to sensible objects, such as the square or circular figures that we draw or make or find in nature. They can be nearly true about them, and the more closely the sensible objects approximate to the mathematical objects the more nearly do these propositions apply to them. We can see from this how natural it is to come to think of the mathematical objects as complete and perfect forms to which the sensible objects can approach closer and closer but can never quite reach, if they are to remain sensible objects. And we can understand how Plato in the *Phaedo* can come to speak of these latter, by a metaphor, as 'trying to be like' the perfect forms.

This, then, is the first stage in Plato's analysis, a stage which is specially characteristic of him and which, as far as we know, he was the first person to reach. The science of mathematics only attains its perfect precision and certainty because, and in so far as, it does not apply to the objects perceived by the senses. But, as it certainly applies to something, that 'something' must belong to a world of non-sensible realities. On the other hand, it does have a certain rough and approximate application to the sensible world, in so far as the objects in that world approximate to the objects of pure scientific knowledge. And it is only in so far as they do this that we can think intelligibly about them at all. We can think about them because they do approximate to the objects of scientific knowledge. But because it is *only* an approximation, the thinking is of an essentially different kind from the scientific knowledge. It is never exact or definite or certain, but is at best only roughly true or true enough for practical purposes, and it is always liable to confusion, error, and contradiction.

The next step is also specially characteristic of Plato, and it is the one to which he probably attached the greatest importance. What light can this analysis of the implications of scientific thought throw on the possibility of a scientific knowledge of morality? At first sight, it might appear that there was not much resemblance. Mathematics was a going concern, and, in spite of theoretical doubts on the part of a few sceptics, it did present a systematic and coherent body of scientific knowledge. It was much more difficult to disbelieve its results than to accept them. And if we accepted them we were bound to believe in the reality of the objects known in it. On moral questions, on the other hand, it seemed far easier to disbelieve in the validity of our judgements, and there was certainly, in fact, much more difference of opinion and much less precision and coherence. Yet if we could, for a moment, bring ourselves to think of the system of moral judgements as a going concern we should find that, in its assumptions and implications, it was much more like the body of mathematical knowledge than would appear at first sight.

If, for instance, we consider Plato's metaphor of 'trying to be like', we shall see that in this field, according to our ordinary assumptions, it ceases to be a metaphor and becomes a literal statement of fact. We are all familiar with the notion of a moral idea to which we human beings can approximate more and more closely, but never completely attain. 'We are none of us perfect', we say glibly. But such a judgement implies the notion of a standard of perfection which we can know at least well enough to see that even the best of us have not completely attained to it. It is only if we assume such a standard that we can say that we are not perfect, and, still more obviously, that one person, though not perfect, is better than another, or one action, though not a complete embodiment of righteousness, is more righteous than a possible alternative. We assume, further, that these ideals are determined for us by the nature of reality. We are not free to make them up just as we like. There is a real right and wrong about them. In other words, they are facts there to be discovered.

What, then, about the doubts and differences of opinion that we find in practice? In the light of our analysis, these need not surprise us, nor need they provide any insuperable difficulty to believing in the objective validity of our moral ideas. As the analogy of mathematical knowledge has shown us, our knowledge of particular sensible objects, in this case the behaviour of particular human beings, can never be certain and definite, and there will always be an element of uncertainty, contradiction and error. Further, if we attempt, as most people do, to study this behaviour by itself, without any clear conception of the ideal standards in the light of which we can judge it, we shall

not have any basis even for such approximation to the understanding of it as we could attain if we went about it the right
way. It is inevitable, therefore, that such thinking would be
confused and indecisive, and that doubts and differences of
opinion would arise, which there would be no way to resolve.
Plato seems to have thought that, if we would study the ideal
forms of morality first, apart from the difficulties that arose
in their practical application, we could reach clear-cut and
definite knowledge of them which would deserve to be called
scientific. We could then in the light of them attain such clearness as the subject-matter would admit about the practical application of these ideals to the behaviour of actual human
beings. He may well have been over-optimistic in this. But, at
any rate, it was an approach that had not yet been tried.

The main point is, however, that Plato had come to the conclusion that the basis of objective reality in our moral judgements lay in these perfect or ideal forms which were never
discovered or realized completely in the world known to
sense-perception. But they were real and knowable in exactly
the same sense as the objects of mathematical science. These
were the kind of objects to which full reality belonged. Where
else could one look for fully real objects such as these is a question on which a word or two will be said later. But it is most
probable that Plato first reached his conception of them by the
considerations of these two fields, the objects of mathematical
science, and the moral ideals or moral qualities which were
assumed in moral judgements. And these are certainly the
clearest and most typical instances by which to illustrate the
sort of things he had in mind and the way he thought about
them.

Before going further, it is necessary to say a word or two
about terminology. In speaking of these fully real objects, he
uses many different expressions. When speaking of any particular instance of them he usually indicates it by the use of the
Greek word for 'itself', as 'the circle itself' or 'justice itself', or
rather, as classical Greek had not yet taken kindly to the use
of the abstract noun, 'the just itself'. He also sometimes speaks
of them generally as 'the things which always remain the same'.
But he soon developed the use of technical terms for these by

the application of two Greek words, whose precise translation needs a word of explanation. These are the words εἶδος (eidos) and ἰδέα (idĕa), which, so far as we can discern, were used absolutely interchangeably. They were, of course, common Greek words, and Plato himself throughout his writings frequently used them in one or other of their various non-technical senses. It is necessary, when reading Plato in the Greek, to remember this and not to assume that this developed theory is implied whenever these words occur. When using them in the technical sense he often, but not invariably, adds a qualifying adjective such as νοητά (noēta), intelligible as opposed to sensible, or ἀσώματα (asōmata), bodiless or immaterial. What he had in mind in choosing the words εἶδος and ἰδέα has been a matter of some controversy, into which it would be impossible to go here. As for the best translations of them, the latter of the two is exactly transliterated by the English 'idea', and hence in the past they have often been spoken of as 'ideas', and the whole theory as the Theory of Ideas. But that is a most unfortunate translation, as 'idea' normally conveys to us something which is not certainly real—'it's just my idea'—but exists only 'in the mind'. And that is just what these objects are not. A better translation, and one which conveys more nearly the suggestion of the Greek words, is 'form'. Hence the modern tendency, which will be followed here, is to speak of them as Forms, and of the theory as the Theory of Forms.

As regards the relation between the Forms and the particular sensible objects, which is such an essential and distinctive feature of the theory, Plato is much more certain of the fact than of the best name to describe it by. In the above account, it has been more than once spoken of as an 'approximation' of the particular objects to the Forms, and Plato uses a somewhat similar metaphor when he speaks in the passage already referred to of the sensible objects 'trying to be like' or 'striving towards' the Form. More often he speaks of the 'presence' of the Form or of 'sharing' or 'participation'. Sometimes he changes the metaphor slightly, and speaks of 'imitation'. The relation of the Form to the particular object is spoken of as the relation of pattern to copy, and in a well-known passage in the *Republic* it is compared to the relation of a sensible object to its shadow or reflection. These varying phrases often appear in different passages of the same dialogue, and Plato makes it clear that he attached comparatively little importance to the exact phrase chosen. Indeed, as he was the first person to call attention to the special character of this relation, it stands to reason that he could not find a precise phrase already assigned to it in the existing vocabulary of his own language.

These, then, are the general characteristics of the theory as it first appears in the dialogues, and, as far as we can discover, they continued to characterize it up to the last stage of Plato's thought. But, of course, as his thought developed, there were some modifications and a great many additions to it. These will be considered later. Before going on to this there still remains, however, the task of seeing how in the first stage it was worked out in detail and applied in different directions to the solution of various problems. To this task we must next proceed.

NOTE ON CHAPTER II

As already explained, the theory discussed in this chapter is never set out or argued systematically by Plato, but is merely referred to for its bearing on some particular problem. Any attempt to set it out systematically must inevitably, therefore, be made for us by ourselves in our own way. I have tried, as it were, to expound it as I thought, from all the indications we can find in the dialogues, Plato might have expounded it to an audience at the present day.

None the less, except for the references to modern science and the quotations from contemporary authors, there is, I think, nothing in my exposition which cannot be verified from passages scattered throughout the dialogues. The criticism of sense-perception can be found in detail in the first part of the *Theaetetus*. It is mainly based here on the experience of taste, smell, and the perception of hot and cold by touch. There is also a reference to dreams. It is also implied in several passages in the *Republic*. For instance, in Book X there is reference to the stick seen bent in water, and to the different shapes seen from different perspectives. The impossibility of real knowledge of what is constantly changing and shifting is argued expressly at the end of the *Cratylus*, and implied in many passages in other dialogues.

The special relation, which I have described as 'approximation', of the objects of sense-perception to the perfect Forms is brought out most clearly in the *Phaedo*, 74, 75. The instance taken there is the mathematical relation of equality, and the contrast is drawn between the absolute equality that we think of in mathematics and the rough, approximate equality which is what we have to be content with in dealing with sensible objects. In the same passage, the parallel between this and the moral ideals is clearly stated when it is said that exactly the same thing applies to absolute justice, holiness, and the other moral qualities. In a later passage there is also mention of 'oneness' and 'twoness' or unity and duality ($\mu o \nu \acute{a} s$, $\delta \nu \acute{a} s$) as instances of the same kind of thing. In Book VII of the *Republic* we get a similar statement of the difference between the mathematical one, and the single sensible object which we never perceive merely as one but also as many at the same time. The instance of geometrical figures is not given in these passages, but in the Parable of the Line in Book VI of the *Republic* we hear of 'the Square itself' or 'the Diagonal itself' of which the diagrams that we draw are merely imperfect imitations. There are other passages, too, and, of course, the point of view is implied throughout. But this will suffice to indicate the kind of evidence on which what I have been saying is based.

3
The Theory of Forms (2)—Developments and Applications

THE CONSIDERATIONS dealt with in the last chapter were certainly at the centre of Plato's mind in developing his theory. But there were other aspects of it which deserve consideration. There are also various difficulties that arise in trying to interpret it in a way that will make it clear to us at the present day. A great many of these difficulties will have to be left unsolved here. There have been, for instance, numerous controversies about points of detail and the interpretation of particular passages. But, with occasional exceptions, these will have to be left unnoticed through limitations of space, even when a satisfactory solution of them does appear possible. Besides that, there are various philosophical difficulties that occur to us in trying to think out Plato's theory for ourselves. To some of them, no doubt, Plato would have had an answer of some sort, and in some cases we can make a plausible conjecture of what this answer would have been. In other cases, even though he might have had an answer, we cannot even guess what it would have been, owing, as previously explained, to the special form in which Plato's work has come down to us. But there are still other cases in which there is no reason to suppose that Plato had any answer to the difficulties at all. It would be absurd to expect him to have thought of all the possible problems that have been raised in the course of two thousand years of subsequent speculation, or to criticize him for not having an answer to every question that we can raise today. This is not always to Plato's disadvantage. For the history of thought has amply shown that a great many problems are always being raised that further reflection shows not to have been real problems at all; and, if we read Plato aright, he can often take us by a direct road to the centre of the question without having to explore all the blind alleys that have been opened up by subsequent speculation. At any rate, there are quite enough problems that Plato and his contemporaries did think of to occupy our full attention.

1. There is one obvious application of the theory which Plato must certainly have had in mind. That is, its application to the general problems of predication, classification and definition. Thinkers before and contemporary with Plato had already begun to ask the question, *What exactly do we imply when we say that this is that?* More especially did they concern themselves with the problem of what was implied by asserting the same thing of a number of different subjects, as in saying that a number of different actions are all just, or a number of different figures are all square. The first thinkers who concerned themselves with these problems raised all kinds of difficulties, some of which have ceased to worry us now, largely because of the work of analysis initiated by Plato. Some of them, indeed, had already ceased to worry him, and are dismissed in the dialogues in which they are mentioned as mere verbal puzzles with no substance in them. But he does take more seriously the general difficulty that was raised by those who asked how a number of different things could also be one, as was implied by calling them all by the same name; and conversely how one thing, e.g. justice, could also become many by being found in a number of different acts. This was an aspect of the general problem of the One and the Many, or unity and multiplicity, which in various forms occupied a good deal of the attention of Greek thinkers.

Plato's general answer, so far as we have taken him at present, was that the one feature, in virtue of which we call a number of things by the same name, was not, strictly speaking, found in the things, but was 'beyond' them. It was to be thought of, not as an identical property found in exactly the same form in all of them, but as a limit towards which they converged to a greater or lesser degree, without ever quite reaching. And, as they would fall short in varying degrees and in different ways, it might well be that it would not be possible, literally, to find a common quality which was absolutely identical in all of them. And yet, once we have conceived the perfect Form, we could see that all these particulars did have a relation to it in virtue of which they fell naturally into a single class or group.

If we try this out in practice, without necessarily accepting Plato's metaphysical theory, we shall find many cases in which it is a very fruitful method of tackling the problem of classification. In other cases, however, it does not seem to work so well. And that raises the question whether we necessarily imply the existence of a perfect Form in every case of classification. In one passage in the *Republic* Plato says, incidentally, that whenever a number of things is called by the same name we postulate a Form. But it is hard to believe that he meant that quite literally. We can make up quite arbitrary classifications, or classifications useful merely for some momentary purpose, on the basis of a feature that has no necessary connexion with the essential nature of the objects classified. We could, for instance, group together all the wheeled vehicles that we observe passing a particular point between two times arbitrarily chosen. We could then, if we liked, invent a name for them all. But it would be impossible to suppose that there is a perfect Form of the objects classified. And it is easy to think of other cases, not quite so extreme as this, which present considerable difficulty. In the *Parmenides*, a dialogue which falls stylistically into the same period as the *Republic* but must certainly have been somewhat later, there is a brief discussion of this point. The interpretation of the dialogue is much disputed, but the general impression from this passage is that Plato had not arrived at any final decision on the question, but was inclined to postulate Forms only of the sort of object, such as moral qualities and mathematical objects and relations, from which we have been illustrating them hitherto. Certainly practically all his own illustrations of them are taken from these fields. The only significant exception is the application to manufactured objects, in this particular case a bed, in Book X of the *Republic*.

In the later developments of his theory, if we can rely on the evidence of his pupil, Aristotle, he did arrive at more definite conclusions on the question. A word will be said about that when we come to consider the final phase of his thought. But we shall probably see reason to suspect that these conclusions were reached not so much by a direct attack on this particular problem, as by a further examination of the nature of the Forms themselves. Once this had been carried out, the particular problem more or less solved itself.

2. A most important point that arises, in connexion with the application of Plato's theory, is the question of the kind of knowledge,[1] or approximation to knowledge, that we can have of the world of sensible objects. It is really the strangest misunderstanding of Plato to represent him, as some modern writers have done, as simply dismissing the sensible world as of no interest. On the contrary, he regarded knowledge and understanding of it as of vital importance, both as a means to the knowledge of the true realities, the Forms, and, even more perhaps, as essential for the conduct of ordinary life. It is true, of course, that we could never have complete or perfect knowledge of it, as we could of the Forms, and therefore the philosopher or lover of knowledge could never find this imperfect knowledge so satisfying as the perfect knowledge of the true realities. It is true, also, that Plato feels the need of giving most of his space to emphasizing the necessity of knowledge of the Forms, not only as more satisfying in itself, but also for the practical conduct of life. That is natural enough, for that was the point on which people needed most explanation and persuasion. But even in the dialogues in which he is most emphatic on this there are plenty of statements of the need for practical experience in addition.

In saying that sensible objects were not fully real, Plato did not, of course, mean that they were just non-existent. For that would mean that they were nothing at all, and that nothing could be said or thought about them. It was just on that point that some lines of Greek thought had got into difficulties by

---

[1] I do not propose to confine the use of the word 'knowledge' to the absolutely complete and certain knowledge which Plato calls ἐπιστήμη (epistēmē). It seems to me much more convenient, and in accordance with English usage, to extend its use to cognition in general. When I want to limit its application I shall use a qualifying adjective.

assuming that there were merely two alternatives, on the one hand complete reality or being, and on the other complete un-reality or non-existence. Plato tried to avoid this by recognizing an intermediate state between complete reality and absolute non-reality which was characteristic of the world of sensible objects. They are described, in the well-known phrase in the *Republic,* 'as tossing about between being and not-being'. Similarly, there are not merely, for him, the two alternatives of complete knowledge and complete ignorance or absence of knowledge. There is also the sort of half-knowledge or ap-proximation to knowledge which we can have of these inter-mediate objects. This is the state of mind that Plato calls δόξα (*doxa*), which is generally translated 'belief' or 'opinion'.

This is not mere sense-perception. As far as we can judge, though there is not much said about it, the mere sensations are for Plato simply a series of fleeting events, and do not in them-selves amount to any sort of cognition at all. But we do reason or think or make judgements about them, and it is that sort of thinking that he is talking about. We have already seen some-thing of its general characteristics. The judgements it arrives at are not absolutely true, but may work well enough for prac-tical purposes. They are roughly or approximately true with a margin of error, which is not merely the result of the limitations of our actual knowledge but is inevitable from the very nature of the objects. Or they may be taken as true from one point of view but not from another, or for some purposes and not for others. It is this sort of thinking which constitutes opinion or belief, δόξα as opposed to ἐπιστήμη, perfect scientific know-ledge. It must be emphasized that the distinction is not at all a distinction between different degrees of subjective certainty in particular cases, but a distinction between the kinds of cognition which are possible. And that finally depends upon the nature of the objects.

A further important point is that Plato does not lump to-gether everything in the sensible world as on just the same level of half-reality, nor all kinds of thinking about it as on the same level of half-knowledge. He recognizes that within this world there are different degrees of approximation to reality, and that some forms of opinion or belief are much nearer true knowledge than others. On the first point, he gives us, as an illustration, the difference between a shadow or a reflection and the sensible physical object whose shadow or reflection it is. It is obvious that, by all the tests of reality previously discussed, shadows or reflections are on a much lower level of reality than their originals. They are more fleeting and impermanent, their observable characteristics are much less definite, and even the degree of existence they have is dependent or derivative. And it is a one-sided dependence at that: for while they could not exist at all without their originals the originals are not in the least dependent on them. These features suggested to Plato that the relation between them might provide, within the sensible world, an analogue of the relation of the sensible world as a whole to the world of Forms.

Now it is obvious that the sort of knowledge that we could have of things such as shadows and reflections would be much vaguer and more uncertain than that which we could have of their originals. That, however, is not a point on which Plato lays much stress. He is more concerned to call attention to the extremely imperfect knowledge that we should have of the originals if we only knew them indirectly through their shadows or reflections and only had direct sensible perception of these latter. We are in substantially the same position if we only know the objects of sense-perception second-hand through someone else's description of them. For the words in which they are described are, in a way, a kind of image or reflection of the things described. In several passages in different dialogues Plato stresses the distinction between our thinking or opinion about sensible objects which is based on our own direct perception of them, and that which is based on a second-hand description of them. So one prescription, at any rate, for making our thinking about sensible objects as correct as it is capable of being is to base it, as far as possible, on our own observation.

There is a further point, which has been of the greatest importance for the subsequent development of thought. In the last book of the *Republic* and in a much later dialogue, the *Philebus*, Plato makes it clear what it is that he regards as the prime condition for making knowledge of the sensible world approximate as closely as possible to the true knowledge of the Forms. And that is the use of precise measurement, 'numbering and measuring and weighing', and the consequent expression of the results in mathematical terms. It is only by that method that we overcome, to some degree, the confusions and contradictions of immediate sense-experience, and rise beyond mere empirical habits of thought to something which approaches—'participates in', as Plato would say—true scientific knowledge. In fact, as far as he would admit scientific knowledge of the sensible world, Plato would echo the words of a modern scientist, 'Science is measurement'.

Plato is not, of course, entirely original in this. The fundamental idea is taken over from Pythagoras and the Pythagoreans, though Plato develops it and applies it in a way which is probably nearer to that of the modern scientist. But the most interesting thing about it is its bearing on subsequent thought. For it certainly shows Plato to have been very much in line with, at any rate, one of the influences that have produced the modern scientific outlook. It has sometimes been said by modern writers that Plato's influence has been unfavourable to the development of natural science as we know it. But this has no basis in the available evidence, which, such as it is, tells all the other way. Certainly, in fact, the century or so immediately following Plato was one of the great ages in the development of natural science, and some branches of it developed for the first time then. What is more, some of the most prominent figures in their development were former pupils of Plato in the Academy. There is no evidence whatever that in following these interests they felt themselves in any way in opposition to Plato. The best known of them is, of course, Aristotle, and, while he criticizes Plato on some points, there is not the slightest hint that in pursuing his biological researches he felt himself to be departing from Plato's teaching. On one point, indeed, on which he criticizes him, many modern scientists would probably feel that Plato was more in the right than Aristotle. That is in the stress that Plato lays, and Aristotle deprecates, on the importance of mathematics for the understanding of the material world. It is noteworthy that some of the founders of modern science in the seventeenth century, such as Kepler and Galileo, mention Plato, among others, by name in this connexion and proclaim themselves followers of his philosophy in opposition to Aristotle's. It is, no doubt, true that Plato was not himself very much interested in research in natural science, though he was evidently well acquainted with the work that was being done. But the idea that his influence was positively hostile to such research is entirely a modern invention.

3 (a). There is another point which is of the greatest interest, and also of the greatest obscurity. That is the question of the relations of the Forms to each other. They have been spoken of hitherto as if they constituted a number of isolated and in-dependent entities, all on a level with each other. But obviously there must be some sort of relation, other than mere co-exist-ence, between them, and between certain Forms the relation must be particularly close. To take but one instance, the Form of Three must have some special kind of relation to the Form of Triangle. And again some Forms seem as if they must be re-garded as sub-species of others. It is clear from various allu-sions, particularly in the *Republic,* that Plato had developed a view on this general question. But the allusions are extremely cryptic and it is far from clear what his view was.

It appears from one passage in the *Republic* that, just as there were different levels among the objects of sense-perception, so there were equally different levels among the objects of pure thought, the Forms. But that is not at all an easy conception to grasp. For, while it is not difficult to see that there might be different degrees of remoteness from perfect reality among the partly real objects of sense-perception, it is very difficult to see how there can be different degrees of perfection among the per-fect objects themselves. It is possible that in this passage Plato is thinking, primarily, not so much of different levels among the real objects themselves as of different levels in our under-standing of them. Indeed, he certainly is thinking of this latter, whether he is also thinking of the former or not. So we may begin with a word or two on this point.

In the first place, the particular mathematical sciences, arith-metic, geometry and the like, are represented as not rising to the highest level of perfect knowledge at which we ultimately aim. One reason for that is that they have to use sensible aids, for instance the diagrams which we draw in geometry, and that fact hampers the exercise of pure thought. I suppose he would say that, as long as we are dependent on the diagrams, there always lingers about our notion of, say, a triangle some sort of idea of it as a figure that 'looks like that', whereas the Triangle Itself does not 'look like' any visible object at all. What is, perhaps, more important is that these sciences always start from ὑποθέσεις (hypotheseis), a word which must not here be translated 'hypotheses' but 'assumptions', things taken for granted without further examination. They take for granted the things given in the preliminary definitions, the various geometrical figures, for instance, and, starting from them as self-evident, they proceed to deduce the different properties of these figures.

Plato did not doubt that the knowledge so attained was perfectly valid scientific knowledge as far as it went. But he was not content with it because he was a philosopher and it is the business of a philosopher to examine assumptions instead of taking them for granted, to see what lies behind them and to carry on this process up to the limits of human thought. Socrates was probably the first person to adopt consciously and explicitly this method of thinking. But it was implicit in most of the work of the Greek philosophers from the beginning, and it plays its part in the development of scientific thought, particularly in mathematics and the sciences that depend on mathematics. The special form it takes there is the demand for ever wider generalization, based on the idea that it marks a progress in understanding whenever we can see two or more apparently different things as instances of some one more general principle. I have heard a physicist describe the task of theoretical science as 'to make one idea grow where there were two before'. And Bertrand Russell in his *Introduction to Mathematical Philosophy* defines the attitude of the mathematical philosopher, as distinguished from the practising mathematician, in these terms: 'Instead of asking what can be defined or deduced from what is assumed to begin with, we ask instead what more general ideas and principles can be found, in terms of which what was our starting-point can be defined or deduced.' This appears to express Plato's demand exactly, and in language not so very different from that which he might have used himself.

So far there does not appear to be any very great difficulty in understanding what Plato had in mind. But the further developments of this are much more complicated and obscure. The first question that arises is whether the above account refers entirely to differences in the degrees of our knowledge and different ways of looking at the same objects, or whether it also implies differences among the objects. Russell, for instance, immediately after the passage just quoted, insists that 'the distinction is one, not in the subject-matter, but in the state of mind of the investigator'. But Plato, believing as he did that in mathematics we were discovering facts about objective reality, could hardly, I think, have accepted this. It seems most probable that, where we should talk of subsuming two or more mathematical concepts under a more general one, he would, at this stage of his thought, think rather of discovering another Form which had 'communion with' or was 'present to' the Forms previously known. At any rate, it seems clear that when he was writing the *Republic* he had some idea of a hierarchy of Forms, some at a higher level than others. And he conceived the progress of knowledge as going behind the first simple Forms that we were dealing with in the particular sciences to those on a higher level which lay behind them, until eventually we arrived at the first principle of all, the ultimate object of thought. And then, in the light of that, we should understand the particular Forms we began with, no longer as isolated entities, but as members of a hierarchical system. It would be vain to attempt to elaborate any more detailed account from the very summary indications given us in the dialogues.

3 (b). On one point, however, something further must be said. There are clear indications in the *Republic* that, when that dialogue was written, Plato had some notion of a supreme first principle, a Form of Forms, as it were, in the knowledge of which ultimate explanation and understanding was to be found. And he calls this first principle by the name of the chief moral category, the Good or, as he sometimes refers to it, the Form of the Good. But his references to it are extremely obscure, and it is very difficult for us to form any clear idea in our own minds of the way in which he thought about it.

It is not so very difficult to understand, in a general way, how that would apply to the various moral qualities and ideals which formed one part of the world of Forms. Courage, justice, piety, and the like are all virtues or good things, but no one of them is the whole of goodness. It is natural to think of them as having something in common which makes them all good, and, on the Platonic theory, that would most naturally be described as their common relation to the Form of good. Even within these limits, the detailed application of the idea is very far from clear. In the passage in which it is first introduced the Good is several times spoken of as that which we aim at before everything else, that without which we can never be satisfied, and that for the sake of which we do everything we do. As we have already seen, something like this is implied in the ordinary Greek use of the word. Yet Plato certainly did not think that the essential nature of the Good consisted in our subjective feelings. Possibly a clue to his meaning may be found if we recall the phrase previously quoted in which the general relation of the particular objects to the Forms is metaphorically described as 'trying to be like them'. So far as we take that phrase seriously, we can see that, from the point of view of the particular sensible object, the one essential fact about all the Forms was that they were what their particulars were ultimately striving to become. We shall see, when considering the later developments of his philosophy, how Plato modified and improved this first vague idea.

That may possibly also give us some sort of clue to the solution of the chief difficulty of this passage. As suggested, the supreme position assigned to the Good is not so difficult to understand when we are considering the Forms of moral qualities and ideals. But that it should also be taken as the ultimate first principle of the mathematical and scientific Forms is a very hard notion indeed. So difficult has it seemed to some scholars that they have tried to raise doubts as to whether Plato really meant that at all. But there is no getting away from it. The statements in the dialogue are quite unequivocal, that the Good is the supreme principle of the whole of the world of Forms, and that it is the final stage of knowledge that we reach when we go behind the assumptions of the particular sciences. But how Plato conceived it we really cannot tell, except for the very slight hint referred to in the preceding paragraph. Probably the nearest analogy in the thought of our own time should be looked for in some form of theistic doctrine, which makes God the supreme source both of the laws of nature and the moral law at the same time. But it is only a very imperfect analogy. For the Good is certainly not God. It is not a personal being, and it is not even soul or mind at all, but rather the supreme object of both the knowledge and the striving of soul.

There has undoubtedly been, in this country, a certain tendency to exaggerate the importance of this particular point for the understanding of Plato's thought, owing to the fact, for which there are very good reasons, that Platonic studies here have been so largely concentrated on the *Republic*. For the *Republic* is the only dialogue in which the Form of the Good as the supreme principle of knowledge and reality appears at all. In earlier dialogues 'good' is mentioned simply as one among many ethical terms for which we must assume a corresponding Form. In later dialogues, so far as there is any indication of a notion of one supreme first principle, it takes quite a different form from this. Altogether it seems reasonable to suppose that, when he wrote the *Republic,* he had adopted this idea as a tentative and provisional way of thinking which in this particular form was subsequently abandoned.

What he never abandoned, however, was the general demand that this particular theory was intended to satisfy. That is the demand that the ultimate metaphysical explanation, whatever form it took, should apply equally to the facts revealed by scientific investigation and the facts referred to in our moral judgements. This combination of a keen interest in the results of the scientific thought of the age and an equally keen interest in the problems of conduct, together with the conviction that our interpretations of both these aspects of human experience must somehow be brought together under a principle common to both, has been characteristic of most of the systems of thought of all ages. The most obvious instances of this are the various forms of theistic doctrine already referred to, particularly the Christian theology. But it is equally characteristic of the various naturalistic explanations, which seek to unify the two by reducing one to the other. We find it, indeed, in most of those who have attained the greatest eminence as thinkers, Spinoza, Kant, Hegel, and the various Idealist philosophers who are influenced by Hegel. So, whether we accept this point of view or not, we must recognize that in adopting it Plato was in the line of the great tradition, of which he was one of the first representatives.

4. One more point remains for discussion, and that is the question of how we come to a knowledge of the Forms. There is not very much said about this. In most passages it seems to be taken as a given fact, which is itself taken as a basis of the proof that there are Forms. There is undoubtedly a good deal of justification for this. If we find that, in fact, we are thinking and coming to conclusions in a certain way, there is not much sense in raising questions about the possibility of our thinking like this. It is a case of *solvitur ambulando.* Certainly the science of mathematics was an accomplished fact, and its possibility hardly needed proof.

None the less there are certain implications of this fact to which Plato seems at times to have given a certain amount of attention. There is a very well-known passage in the *Phaedo,* in which he seeks to apply these implications to the proof of the immortality of the soul. He starts here from the fact that in observing sensible objects we are able on reflection to recognize that they approximate to some perfect Form but always fall short to a greater or lesser degree. The particular instance which he takes here is the comparison between absolute mathematical equality and the rough approximate equality that we observe in the objects of sense-perception. It seems, then, as if in some sense we must be already acquainted with the perfect Form before we can judge that the sensible objects fall short of it, though in our actual experience in this life it is the acquaintance with objects through sense-perception that comes first in point of time. But, as we have already seen, we do not find the perfect Form *in* the sensible objects because it is not there. He compares the experience rather to being reminded of some object that we have previously known by the sight of another object that is something like it but not identical, as when a portrait reminds us of the original. And he draws the conclusion that we must have become acquainted with the originals of which we are reminded, the perfect Forms, in a previous state of existence before we entered our bodies. This notion of pre-existence, combined with certain other arguments, provides, it is suggested, some proof of the immortality of the soul.

It has sometimes been doubted whether, or how far, Plato meant this argument to be taken literally. It has been suggested, for instance, that it is an expression in figurative or metaphorical language of a more abstract argument, on the lines that the capacity of the mind to grasp the Forms at all, which cannot be done through the bodily senses, shows that it has capacities which cannot be described in terms of the body or of physical occurrences, and that therefore it must be supposed to have a substantial, non-corporeal existence of its own. It cannot be said that this is impossible. Plato does sometimes express a general truth in more concrete figurative form, though it is generally much more obvious than it is here when he is doing so. But there seems really nothing in the passage itself to make us doubt that he intended it literally, at the time he wrote it. He may not, however, have regarded himself as finally and definitely committed to this view. The general suggestion that the process of acquiring knowledge in these fields is really a process of remembering what we had known in a previous existence outside of the body is first put forward in the *Meno*. And there he says that he is not at all prepared to insist on the doctrine in this precise form, as long as the possibility of the process of acquiring this kind of knowledge somehow or other is recognized.

These, then, are some of the main points that arise in connexion with the developments and applications of the fundamental doctrine. There are, no doubt, many other problems that might occur to us, but there is no point in speculating about what Plato might have said on them, if he had had anything to say at all. There remains one further matter to which the theory of Forms has some application, though a good deal that Plato says about it has no necessary connexion with the theory at all. That is the moral, social, and political theory, which is treated by Plato, as it would have been by most Greek thinkers of the time, as fundamentally a single subject. This, however, is a matter of sufficient importance to need treatment by itself.

4

Moral and Political Theory (1)

THE TREATMENT of this subject must necessarily at this stage centre, in the main, round the *Republic,* the most read and the most commented on of all Plato's dialogues. It is here that we get the nearest approach to the systematic exposition of a formed doctrine that we find anywhere in his writings. Adumbrations of this doctrine are, however, found earlier, particularly in the *Gorgias,* also one of the key dialogues for the understanding of Plato's thought. But here they are merely indicated, and put forward rather as a matter of faith than of reasoned proof. In the *Republic* similar ideas are developed in detail and presented as the conclusion of a lengthy and systematic argument.

In the *Gorgias,* as already indicated in a previous chapter, we are in the main occupied with the presentation and criticism of one particular form of the argument for moral scepticism. But we are left at the end with certain positive ideas which emerge from the critical work of the dialogue. There is, firstly, the general faith in the reality of moral values, which is implied throughout and reaffirmed in a passage of moving eloquence at the close. Secondly, there is the insistence that, if these moral values are real, they must provide the standards by which everything, in the final resort, is judged. In particular, they provide the standard by which the value of political activity, the organization and government of the community, is tested. The true statesman, we are told, is the man who leaves the citizens better men than he found them. And finally there is the suggestion that the kind of knowledge that is necessary for carrying out this task is to be found in philosophical reasoning. It is the main object of the *Republic* to justify this faith by systematic argument.

The *Republic* begins with a discussion of the meaning of a Greek word which is generally translated 'justice'. But this translation, though it fits well enough into certain contexts, is really misleading. For the implications of the Greek word, though they include those of the English, are wider in extent, and cover almost the whole field of what we should describe as our duty towards our neighbour, or proper behaviour towards other people. Even more clearly, perhaps, the opposed terms (ἄδικος, ἀδικία, conventionally translated 'unjust' and 'injustice') really imply a general lack of moral scruple and disregard of other people's rights or interests. In many passages 'unscrupulous' is a better translation of ἄδικος than 'unjust'. In fact, in discussing this virtue we are not far from a discussion of the whole meaning and basis of morality, so far as it refers to the behaviour of one person to others.

There is some reason to believe that Book I of the *Republic* was written at an earlier date than the rest of the dialogue and used subsequently as an introduction. Certainly it follows the lines with which we are familiar in the earlier dialogues, its results are negative and critical only, and at the end even Socrates himself is left unsatisfied. But it serves its purpose by showing the intellectual situation which gave rise to the need for a deeper and more positive discussion, and the challenge to this is taken up in the rest of the dialogue. It is suggested that we shall understand better what 'justice' is if we examine it in its working in the life of a community, before trying to see what it implies in the way of a state of mind of the individual. And it is to the analysis of the nature of a community that Plato now turns. We must beware, by the way, in this connexion of the persistent mistranslation of πόλις (*polis*) as 'state'. Literally it means 'city', which the Greek regarded as the highest and most developed form of organized community. But if we consider the way in which we use the word 'state' we shall see that it often has for us implications and suggestions that the Greek word has not. On the other hand, of course, 'city' equally does not mean to us just what the corresponding word meant to the Greeks. To express the argument in modern terms, therefore, it is better to use some general term such as 'community', which I have employed here.

In the light of the Theory of Forms it is easy to understand the direction from which Plato approaches his examination of the nature of a community. His first and main concern throughout the greater part of the dialogue is to construct a picture of the ideal or perfect city, a 'pattern in Heaven' as he calls it, in the light of which we can understand communities as we actually find them. It is important to remember what this implies for him. As an ideal it is not something which is found in any existing community, and in the nature of things it can never be realized in its complete perfection in practice, any more than we can ever draw or construct a mathematically straight line. It must never, therefore, be discussed as a practical programme of immediate legislation. But nothing could be more fallacious, in Plato's view, than to suggest that an ideal which cannot be fully realized in practice is therefore of no practical bearing. On the contrary, a clear conception of the ideal is the one essential condition of effective action. Without it we have no standard by which to judge of existing communities or their constitutions and no clear directive by which we can guide our efforts at reform. Our task, if we are ever in a position to carry it out, is to try to approximate as nearly as we can to the ideal with the material at our disposal. Plato compares this to the work of a portrait painter who tries to make a picture as like the original model as he can, though it can never be quite identical with it. And this illustration suggests another point. The painter needs for his task, not only the knowledge of his original, but also the practical understanding of his materials and the technical ability to use them. So, too, the statesman or reformer must first of all have a clear vision of the ideal. But to apply that he needs also practical experience and knowledge of the conditions in which he has to work. This is insisted on several times in the *Republic,* though naturally, as few would be likely to deny it, there is much less stress laid on it than on the need for knowledge of the ideal. But to picture Plato, as has sometimes been done, as constructing a theoretically perfect state in the recesses of his own mind and then supposing that it can be applied ready-made to any existing community without regard to the circumstances is a complete mis-representation for which there is no justification.

This method, the method of ideals as we may call it, is one of Plato's most characteristic contributions to thought about human affairs. It is easy to see how it arises from his general notion of the structure of reality as set out in the Theory of Forms. We cannot necessarily assume that every ideal, as formulated, is strictly and literally a Form, though it would certainly have to be deduced from, or dependent on, a Form in some way. That, however, is not important as far as the application of the method goes. What is of importance is to note the way in which the ideal community is conceived. In one sense it might be said that it was not an ideal community if we mean by that a community of perfect individuals. It is not meant as a picture of the society of the saints in Heaven. It takes individual human beings as they are by nature, and assumes, what all experience suggests, that they are born different with different capacities and different temperaments and different degrees of intelligence. It then asks what is the best conceivable form in which a community of such people could be organized. It is the ideal organization of actual people. Or it might, perhaps, be described as an attempt to picture the utmost that could be got out of the given human material by a perfect education and organization.

How does Plato arrive at his notion of the ideal? There is one passage in which he speaks of 'taking hints from what Homer called the "divine and godlike" element which exists in actual human beings'. But the main key to an understanding of his method must be looked for in his actual practice. And when we look at that we find that he begins by asking what the function or purpose of a community is. And when he has arrived at that he goes on to examine the form that the community would have to take for that function to be fulfilled with a hundred per cent efficiency. Now, the function of a community is to satisfy the needs of its individual members: 'it is our need that will create it', as he says. And it is necessary for that because the individual is not capable of supplying all his needs for himself by his own unaided efforts, but requires the co-operation of others to which he contributes his share in return. Plato begins, therefore, with a little sketch, which might serve as an introduction to any text-book of classical economics, of the principle of division of labour, and shows how essential this is for the effective provision of even the most elementary necessities.

So far as this is applied to the satisfaction of ordinary economic needs no one, in his time or ours, would seriously question it. But he carries it further. For, just as the needs of human beings are by no means confined to the provision of the means of physical life, so their mutal dependence on each other does not stop short at that point. And the principle of division of labour, which expresses this mutual dependence and which we recognize as the condition of efficiency in supplying our physical necessities, must be applied also to our further needs. The first shock to conventional Greek opinion is given when he applies it to the provision of a military force for purposes of defence. For it was still held in principle that the defence of the city was the duty of every citizen, though in practice most Greek states were coming to rely more and more on the superior efficiency of the professional soldier. But Plato goes further still, and applies it to the highest function of all, that of ruling or directing the state. Just because this is the most difficult and most important duty of all, it must, if it is to be done properly, be entrusted to those with the greatest capacity for it, who will devote the whole of their attention to it. And most of the rest of the dialogue is occupied by a consideration of the selection and training of the rulers of the ideal city.

Ruling, then, appears as one function among others in the community, much the most important and difficult, no doubt, but still coming under the general principle of the division of labour for the mutual satisfaction of each other's needs. The special functions of the ruler include, of course, the ordinary administrative duties which fall to the lot of those in authority in any community, and require the practical capacity and careful attention necessary to carry them out efficiently. But much more than that is needed. For the highest function of the ruler is to set the moral standards of the community. As was suggested in an earlier chapter, there will in practice always be in any community some people who have a much greater degree of influence in this respect than the rest. And Plato, it seems, wants this explicitly recognized and the community organized so that those most fitted to exercise this influence should come to the top. It must be added that the chief means by which this influence is exercised is education. And perhaps the most important function of the rulers is the establishment and preservation of the right system of education.

A good deal of space is devoted to the selection, education, and organization of these rulers, or 'guardians' as Plato's word for them is usually translated. We can deal here only with the most general features of this account.

The first stage is the selection of the members of the army, which is to be recognized as a specialized vocation. The superior efficiency as a fighting force of a professional army is the first consideration to be put forward. But Plato is very emphatic that the power that lies in the hands of the only armed forces in the community cannot safely be left to those who are merely good fighters. He demands for them, therefore, high moral and intellectual qualities, and an education and training calculated to develop these. It is not surprising therefore, and would, in any case, seem quite natural to ordinary Greek opinion, that the rulers are selected from the ranks of the soldiers. For one thing no one has been admitted to the ranks of the soldiers unless he has at any rate shown the possibility of developing into a good ruler. And, in addition, we may take this as a recognition by Plato of the vital necessity for the rulers of a community to have control of the organized physical force in it. At every stage, then, the members of the army are submitted to a careful process of selection for promotion and the pick of them reach the highest position of supreme rulers.

The selection at every stage is to be purely on merit. The rulers are certainly not an hereditary caste. Plato does, however, believe that innate qualities tend to be transmitted by inheritance, so that, once the original selection has been made, the majority of the future rulers will be found among the children of those already in that position. But that does not give them any kind of prescriptive right. Those who do not show themselves fit for the position are sent to some other kind of work, and, conversely, promising children from other classes are picked out to be trained as soldiers and rulers. *La carrière ouverte aux talents* is a fundamental principle of the *Republic*, with the proviso that the talent, or at any rate the possibility of it, must be recognized early if it is to receive the education necessary for its proper development. It is worth noting that Plato was sufficiently in advance of his time to apply the same principle to women, who, if they show the necessary qualities, are to be given the same training and the same chance to rise to the highest positions in the state as men. If later writers speak truly, he followed his own principles in practice and admitted a few women of exceptional ability to study in the Academy.

But all the natural qualities which he demands—quickness of understanding and learning, retentiveness of what is learnt, courage, self-control, firmness of purpose, and the rest—are of little avail unless they are developed and directed by the right education. Indeed, he asserts, in a well-known passage, that it is these very qualities which, if they are turned in the wrong direction, are capable of doing the greatest harm. And he devotes careful attention to the proper system of training for his soldiers and rulers. In their youth they follow the conventional Greek education, with a strenuous, but not too specialized, physical training, and a study of the current literature, in the main the stories of the gods and heroes told by the poets and song-writers. It is from this literature that, without direct precept, the young people absorb insensibly their ideas of good and evil and the proper conduct of life in general. Looking at it from this point of view, Plato finds much to criticize in the established body of literature. Certainly some of the stories told by the earlier poets would be very far from edifying, if they are regarded as presenting a picture of the gods and heroes whom we are supposed to worship or to admire and make our models. He, therefore, proposes to exercise a very drastic censorship of this literature, and to cut out all passages which represent these objects of our reverence or admiration as behaving in an undesirable manner. He even extends his restrictions to the form in which both the literature and the music which accompany it are to be presented.

This, however, is only a beginning. It lays a good foundation, in so far as it inculcates a general outlook or point of view which is accepted almost as a matter of habit. But for the rulers, above all people, it is necessary to have not only habits of right behaviour but a rational understanding of what it is all about. So this early training is followed by a prolonged course of study in the mathematical sciences, interspersed with intervals of practical work in subordinate positions of responsibility. These mathematical studies are incidentally recommended as being of some practical value. But their main purpose is to lead the student gradually to look beyond the sensible objects to the non-sensible world, the pure mathematical objects which are the most elementary instances of the Forms. These studies, then, are the prelude to the final stage, the concentrated study of philosophy, or 'dialectic' as Plato calls it, which leads up to a comprehensive view of the nature of reality in the light of the supreme principle, the Form of the Good. This last stage is not completed till about the age of thirty-five. And those who have passed successfully through all these stages now spend the next fifteen years of their lives in the higher executive work of administering the city. At the age of fifty they are released from these day-to-day duties, and allowed to devote the greater part of their time to the pursuit and contemplation of the eternal truths. But they are still required to exercise a general supervision over the running of the state, in which they constitute the supreme authority.

We are not yet at the end of the conditions that Plato lays down to secure the proper exercise of their functions by the rulers and the soldiers. Even the most careful selection and the best of training require to be supplemented by a system of organization which will rule out certain possibilities of the misuse of their powers. Not that rules and institutions by themselves could be effective to restrain the rulers if they had the will to break them. If they have been rightly selected and rightly trained they will themselves wish to live according to the general principles that Plato lays down. But he feels that even these best of men need the support of an established system or way of life, which will shut out the possibility of certain insidious temptations which might on occasions be too much even for them.

The way of life laid down for them is, therefore, extremely austere. They live communally in barracks, owning no private property of any kind, and receiving their rations and the other necessities of life from the rest of the citizens, in just sufficient amount to keep them in full health and strength for the efficient discharge of their duties. Even a private family life is denied to them. Those of the proper age are ceremonially mated from time to time under the direction of the supreme authorities, and the children are brought up in communal nurseries without knowing or being known by their parents. It is these last provisions which seem to us at the present day the most far-fetched and repellent. They would not, perhaps, have seemed so startling to the Greeks. There is a certain amount of evidence that ideas of this kind had been in the air some time before Plato wrote, and certain practices in the Spartan state, while not going as far as this, certainly went a great deal further than anything we should contemplate nowadays. But, in any case, Plato's provisions must be regarded as an attempt, in an extreme form, to guard against the familiar evils of nepotism and family rivalry. In general, the whole scheme is aimed at the removal of any possible rival claims either on the attention or the loyalty of the guardians. They must live wholly for the service of the community, and must have no selfish or particular interests which could possibly set them against either each other or the rest of their fellow-citizens.

There is, however, one interest, though hardly what we usually mean by a selfish interest, which does appeal to them more than the work of ruling. And that is the pursuit of truth for its own sake by philosophical thinking. If they consulted only their personal inclinations, they would devote themselves to this rather than to anything else. And that for Plato is the great safeguard against the danger that his rulers might fall into that subtlest of temptations, which may beset even the most devoted public servant, of coming to love power for its own sake. He says epigrammatically that the only people who can safely be entrusted with absolute power are those who know a better kind of life, which they would really rather pursue. And that is one of the grounds for his famous dictum that a community will never be properly governed unless its rulers are philosophers. It is not, however, the sole ground, and it is worth considering a little more in detail what this dictum implies.

We first hear of the idea at a very early stage, when it is a question of the original selection of those who are to be trained as soldiers. They must be, we are told, not only strong and active, spirited and courageous, but also 'philosophical' by nature. This obviously does not mean, at this stage, that they must be finished philosophers. It refers rather to a general natural tendency which, if it is strong enough, makes them capable of being educated to become such. We must remember, of course, that the Greek word of which our own 'philosopher' is an almost exact transliteration had not yet acquired the specialized meaning which it has for us. It was in process of acquiring it, but it still retained some of the associations of its derivation, and referred in the first instance rather to a direction of one's interest than to any actual attainment. In other words, it means primarily, as its derivation implies, one with a love of or desire for knowledge and wisdom, which can, of course, show itself before much actual knowledge is acquired. We should think, perhaps, of a person who is by nature of an active and inquiring mind, always wanting to find things out and to understand the why and the wherefore of them. It is because this desire to know and to understand can only be finally and completely satisfied by the knowledge of the true realities, the Forms, that we can come later to use the term 'philosophers' specially for those who have come within reach of attaining this knowledge. And it is not till they have reached this stage that they are qualified to be rulers.

It is quite clear that Plato believed that the supreme rulers must be not merely of a philosophical temperament, but trained metaphysicians with a grasp of the ultimate nature of reality. They must be able to think in terms of the perfect Forms, the real ideals, in the light of which they have to understand the empirical facts of the situation and guide their policy. But we can go a little further than this in filling in the details. We get frequent references throughout the account of their long system of training to selection tests which are applied at every stage to pick out those who are to proceed further. The implication of that seems to be that at each stage there will be a certain number who get so far and no further. Thus we may suppose that, just as in mathematical sciences there will be some who may make quite competent mathematicians, but are not capable of the philosophical thinking which will take them behind the assumptions of mathematics, so in the study of political affairs there will be some who can grasp the notion of the ideal community and use it as the ὑπόθεσις or assumption of their political thinking, but cannot rise beyond this to the ultimate principle of reality, the Form of the Good. Such men will occupy, no doubt, an important position in the hierarchy, but will not rise to the top. For, while the stage of knowledge that they have reached may work well enough as a guide in practice for the work they have to do, there is no sure and certain basis of it except in the understanding of its relation to reality as a whole. They must always, therefore, work under the final control of those who have attained this supreme knowledge. We have no means of knowing whether, at the time of writing, Plato thought that he himself had attained this stage. He certainly would not have believed that it was capable of being set out in a written dialogue. But it is quite clear that it was for him the ideal which must be attained if our knowledge is to be complete and certain.

It is not surprising that Plato believed that the qualities which make a true philosopher will be found comparatively rarely among human beings, and that those who possess them will stand out as exceptional people. It must be remembered that he is very far from thinking that intellectual ability, in any restricted sense, is sufficient by itself alone, though it is, of course, one of the prime necessities. But equally necessary are some of what we should more naturally describe as moral qualities. We shall never, for instance, however clever we are, except occasionally by accident, arrive at true conclusions unless we care more about getting at the truth than about anything else, if we are afraid to face unpleasant facts or to maintain views that might be unpopular, if we are swayed by selfish interests or partisan prejudice, if we shrink from or get angry at anything to which we are not accustomed, or if we are too lazy or self-indulgent to keep up the efforts which are demanded. The free-dom from such weaknesses is necessary if we are to pursue the study profitably at all, and, as it proceeds, further good quali-ties are developed. Above all, it gives us a true sense of propor-tion, an appreciation of how small in the light of the eternal verities our petty personal ambitions and desires are. At the same time, once we have had the vision of the ideal, we shall see all our personal activities in the light of it and guide them accordingly. The general result of the argument is that the vocation for the pursuit of philosophy demands rare qualities both of intellect and of temperament intimately combined, and those who have not these qualities had better leave the study of philosophy alone. His idea has many points of resemblance to the Catholic doctrine of vocation, which regards the reli-gious life as the highest form of life possible for man, and yet holds that it would be positively wrong for those who have not the vocation for it to attempt to live it.

This idea of vocation, indeed, is central in Plato's whole pic-ture of the ideal community, and applies just as much to the farmers, craftsmen, traders, and the like, who supply the mate-rial needs of the community, as to the guardians. We are not told much about the position of this class of producers. But there are no grounds for the suggestion that has sometimes been made that Plato ignored them because he despised them and thought them of no importance. Such an idea would be quite contrary to what he says himself about the proper atti-tude of the rulers to the producers. He states emphatically that they must never think of them as bondsmen whom they can use merely to satisfy their own ends. They are fellow-citizens who have the special function of providing the material necessities, in return for the protection and guidance which it is the func-tion of the rulers to give. His community exists for the one just as much as for the others, and it is its object to provide the maximum possible happiness for all alike. Why Plato does not go into details about the position of the producing class is doubtless because he felt that the first essential was to secure the right men and the right organization for the rulers, and that then the rest of the organization of the community could safely be left to them.

We are not, however, without certain indications of the position of the producing class as Plato pictured it. It is not at all likely that the absolute community of property and of family relations was meant to apply to them. There would certainly not have been the same necessity for it as in the case of the supreme rulers. It is quite clear that they would not be required to submit themselves to the same austerities as the guardians and that their material standards of living would be considerably higher, though extremes of wealth or poverty would not be allowed. The modern reader, by the way, must beware of the description, which is sometimes used, of this class as the 'workers' or the 'working class', terms which have in modern English political and social implications which would be very misleading if applied to Plato. This class would include everyone concerned in the work of supplying material needs, what we should call nowadays 'business men' just as much as the 'workers'. But in fact, of course, Plato was not thinking in terms of a modern industrial society divided into 'employers' and 'workers' at all, but rather of a society, in the main, of small farmers and independent craftsmen and traders.

As for the happiness of this class, that would be partly found in the satisfaction of their material needs, and also in the peace and security that the vigilant watchmanship of the guardians would bring them. It would also be found in the fact that each one was working at the job for which his natural capacities most suited him. And, as modern investigations into vocational guidance have emphasized, that is certainly a great source of happiness, or at any rate of the avoidance of a great deal of unhappiness. Nor, if Plato's ideal was realized, would they necessarily feel any dissatisfaction in being deprived of political power. It is one of the most inexcusable misrepresentations of Plato's ideal society to picture it as a state in which a large body of unwilling subjects is held down by force by armed rulers. Of course, as in all communities, force might have to be used from time to time against individual recalcitrants. But it is one of the cardinal features of the ideal state that in all classes there should be, in Plato's phrase, agreement about who should rule and who should be ruled. Furthermore, in a later passage he expresses his belief that the mass of people, once they had been brought to realize what sort of persons the philosopher-guardians would be, would be quite ready to accept their rule and guidance.

This is important, because it throws light on the question, on which much misunderstanding has arisen, of the degree of moral enlightenment of which he thought the unphilosophic mass of people were capable. It is clear that the highest development of this was only possible for the true philosophers. They alone could have the clear understanding of the true nature of the good, which could on the one hand provide a firm basis for the discernment of what was right and what wrong in practice, and on the other give the strength of conviction necessary to withstand all the influences from within and without which might cloud the judgement and deflect the will. It is they, therefore, who must be finally responsible for setting the moral standards of the community. But that does not mean that the rest of the community is made up of entirely passive, non-moral creatures who require to have the most elementary idea of right and wrong imposed on them from above. On the contrary, it would seem that everyone, or nearly everyone, has some feeling of right and wrong, and some sense of a duty to the community. But in the great majority it is neither clear enough nor continuous enough to guide them unaided. It does, however, make them conscious of the need for guidance, and it is because of that that they will respond to the leadership of the philosopher-rulers, once they have been brought to realize what it implies. The principle of division of labour, then, as applied to the work of the ruler meets a felt need of the whole community just as much as when it is applied to the provision of our material necessities.

I have, of course, expressed this argument in my own terms in the light of modern discussions. But there is nothing in it that is not clearly implied by what Plato says. In his unequivocal demand for authoritative moral leadership from above he certainly goes much further than most of us would be prepared to go at the present day, and there is much that could be fairly criticized in his presentation of the case. It would be out of place to attempt this here. But any criticism would miss the point if it failed to recognize that in fact very few people do or can guide their conduct continuously by their own unaided 'inner light'. We all, or nearly all, depend to a greater or lesser degree on the support and guidance of authority, whether it is the authority of a particular person or body of persons or of a generally accepted moral code. Plato may be criticized for exaggerating and formalizing this. But he cannot be justly criticized for recognizing it at all.

5
Moral and Political Theory (2)

WE GET then a clear picture of Plato's notion of the ideal society. He arrives at it by developing to its ideal form the characteristic which he takes to be the fundamental characteristic of any organized society, namely the mutual dependence of its members on one another, so that together they form a unity. A unity, but not a uniformity: for it contains the greatest degree of diversity within itself. Each member has a special contribution of his own to make in accordance with his natural capacities, and together they form a society bound together in mutual friendliness and co-operation. Such a society is not only good and efficient as a society, but provides for its individual members the best, and ultimately the most agreeable, life that is possible to them. This is one stage in Plato's answer to the challenge to show that morality is 'natural'. For morality consists in the rules of behaviour that are necessary to make life in such a society possible. And life in such a society affords the most complete satisfaction of the needs of human nature.

It is not altogether surprising that, trying them by the standard of this ideal, Plato regarded all existing Greek states as falling short, not only of the absolute ideal, but even of the approximations to it that might be attained. Wherever he looked he found, in a greater or lesser degree, dissension and strife within each city, and little trace even of an effort to attain the unity which he regarded as the first essential of a well-organized society. Modern readers may well feel that Plato lays an exaggerated stress on the need for perfect unity. We feel that some degree of difference of opinion and opposition is a condition of development and progress. But we should have to recognize that this is only true within very definite limits. A community divided by irreconcilable differences cannot be in a healthy state. And in ancient Greece differences very readily became irreconcilable. Plato was, of course, speaking of the ideal state of things, and would, presumably, not have ruled out the possibility that in the existing imperfect communities some degrees of conflict might occasionally not be entirely undesirable. Yet, if we consider the actual conditions of his day, we should probably come to feel that he might well be excused for not having much faith in this method, and for feeling that, even in the existing communities, dissension was producing nothing but evil. It would indeed be hard, or impossible, in fourth-century Greece to point to any actual case in which conflict within a city was, in fact, leading to a better state of society.

What particularly impressed Plato was the continual state of conflict between classes. Every city of his time, as he says, was not one city but two, the city of the rich and the city of the poor. And that was the primary evil that his ideal organization was intended to remove.

We have, in the *Republic,* a long discussion of the chief existing types of state, from the point of view of their relation to the ideal state. They are arranged in descending order of merit, and, in order to give a concrete picture of their relation, Plato describes it in terms of an actual historical process of degeneration. This device of presenting the results of an analysis in the form of an historical account is used by Plato elsewhere, and is familiar to us in the work of many subsequent writers down to our own day. There is no reason at all to suppose that Plato was not fully aware of what he was doing, or that he believed that, in fact, changes from one system of government to another took place necessarily, or even normally, in that order. He was well acquainted with the history of his own and other Greek cities, and was quite well aware that in fact changes had taken place in every conceivable order. Further, of course, the account of the stages of degeneration begins from the ideal city which had never in fact existed, even in an approximation. So there is no ground for taking this account as an attempt to arrive at a law of historical development by generalization from actual experience, though, of course, his analysis is illustrated throughout from his knowledge of actual historical situations.

What is of particular interest in this account is his constant attempt to trace back the adoption of this or that form of government to psychological causes, to the dominance of this or that state of mind in the community concerned. He is thinking particularly of the dominant standards of value, the ends which the public opinion of the community regards as most worth pursuing. This, more than anything else, he thinks, will determine the form that the system of government takes. Thus, any city in which the acquisition of wealth is regarded as the natural aim of human endeavour will inevitably tend towards an oligarchy, the concentration of political power in the hands of the wealthy. This is not, however, the first stage of degeneration. That is represented by what he calls the timocratic state, of which Sparta was the outstanding example. This is the state in which prestige and power, honour and glory, are accepted as the highest values. These things are found most readily in military achievements, so that power in the state tends to fall into the hands of the fighting men and success in war to be regarded as the highest object of endeavour. This is just what is wrong with it. Yet it is not wholly an ignoble aim. At the least, it calls for a good deal of personal courage, devotion, and self-denial, of duty, order, and discipline, all good things in themselves as far as they go. Even in our own day, repellent though most of us find the Spartan state, we can still thrill at the story of Thermopylae. But, none the less, it is a fundamentally false ideal, and the pursuit of it involves the neglect of the true values.

Further, it marks the first stage in the break-up of the unity of the state. For the warrior class, who in the good state looked on the rest of the citizens as, in Plato's words, 'free men and friends and providers of their necessities' in return for the protection they gave them, now come to treat the producers as serfs and dependants, existing merely for the sake of their rulers. And even the virtues of this society have no sure basis. For they are instilled merely by the force of discipline, and there is no philosophical understanding of the reasons for them. Such a society, therefore, has the seeds of instability in it from the first, and any change of circumstances may let in other, still lower, impulses.

We get the next stage, then, when ambition and the desire for honour and glory give place to the pursuit of wealth as the chief aim of the society, and the timocracy becomes the oligarchy or plutocracy. This is condemned entirely by Plato. It infringes the fundamental principle of the good society, that every function within it should be performed by those most fitted by character and training for it. It puts political power into the hands of the wealthy, and that is bad for two reasons. The possession of wealth is no test at all of the qualities and knowledge necessary for a ruler. And, what is of even more importance, it gives the rulers private interests of their own which set them in opposition to each other and to the rest of the citizens, and make it impossible for them to rule in the interests of the whole community. Not only is such a result bad in itself, but it makes this constitution, also, inherently unstable. Wealth gives power and power is used to acquire more wealth, with the result that both tend to be concentrated in fewer and fewer hands, the conflict between classes becomes ever greater, and an eventual explosion is almost inevitable. This has obvious points of resemblance to the Marxian analysis. And Plato adds to it a piece of observation, which experience even in modern times has done much to confirm, that the main source of revolution is to be found, not so much among those who have always been poor as among those who have been well-to-do and have subsequently fallen or been driven into poverty. It may be noted how much more directly and obviously this analysis applies to an ancient Greek city than to a modern community. For the Greeks, and indeed the ancient world in general, never developed or even conceived the possibilities of an expanding economy such as we know, in which by improvements in the processes of production the total amount of wealth can go on increasing almost indefinitely. There were certain possibilities of that in the ancient world, but only within very narrow limits. Beyond these limits anyone who wanted to increase his wealth could only do so by, directly or indirectly, taking it from someone else.

But Plato's chief difference from Marx is to be found in his belief that, in the final analysis, these results are due to the attitude of mind of the members of the community, particularly those in authority, rather than to the institutions. Of course the two act and react on each other. But the basic influence lies in the former. So oligarchical institutions are to be regarded as the expression of the belief that wealth is the thing most worth pursuing. But it is really that belief also which gives rise to the revolt against oligarchy on the part of the dispossessed. Plato, therefore, has no faith in the revolution of the masses as the solution of the evils of the plutocratic state. It leads only to a lower order of state still—democracy.

It is important to try to grasp, without being too much prejudiced by modern controversies, the reasons for Plato's strong objection to democracy as he knew it. In the first place, there is the fundamental objection that is implied in his whole treatment of it, that it contradicts the essential feature of the good state, the principle of division of labour. More obviously than any other constitution it denies that the work of ruling the community demands any special qualities or any special knowledge or even any special concentration of attention or interest on it. Of course, even in a democracy the technical specialist was accorded a certain degree of respect on his special subject. But in the higher decisions of policy everyone was supposed to speak with equal authority. In Plato's view, however, these were the most important and the most difficult decisions of all, and therefore demanded the highest degree of intelligence, knowledge and disinterestedness. Democracy, in which the final word on any matter of importance was very jealously reserved to the assembly of the whole people, rested on a denial of this and an angry rejection of any idea of special qualifications being necessary.

If we ask, then, on what principle the democratic constitution rests, the only answer is that there is no principle. The only accepted common aim is the negative one of preventing any particular person or body of persons from getting more authority than anyone else. That is why Plato puts it so low in the scale. Even in an oligarchy there is some idea of an aim to be pursued, which calls for some degree of self-control and concentration on a purpose, even though it is a wrong purpose. A democracy is essentially aimless. The dominance of this merely negative purpose means that there is no recognized person or body of persons with any special degree of responsibility for setting the direction of the whole community.

But that does not mean, as the democratic idealists would like to think, that everyone contributes equally to the formation of a common purpose. The great majority will never give the thought and attention that is necessary for this. So in practice the leadership always tends to fall to those who, like the popular orators, are most skilful in the arts of appealing to the emotions of the crowd, and in particular, of exploiting the jealousy and fear and suspicion which Plato sees as the dominant emotions of a democracy. It is impossible for anyone who has to work by such methods to keep hold of any ideals he may have had, so that there is always the tendency for the chief influence to be exercised by those who, in the American phrase, are 'not in politics for their health', and for a democracy to become the paradise of the unscrupulous political adventurer.

Finally, the democracy fails, just as much as the oligarchy, to secure unity and harmony between the different classes. It must be remembered that, so far as we know, the Greek democratic parties had no considered policy of social reconstruction, such as Plato thought essential to transcend the conflict between classes. They did not question the existing economic system, which allowed great differences of wealth to develop. But, when these had developed, there was a constant tendency to regard the rich as potential enemies, and to subject them, over and above the ordinary process of taxation, to the constant risk of arbitrary spoliation and confiscation, very often on the initiative of unscrupulous politicians or professional informers, who could be sure of making something out of it themselves. To treat anyone as a potential enemy is the surest way of making him one, even if he was not before. So democracy, which begins as a reaction against the evils of the class war, ends by intensifying them.

We do not know enough to say with certainty how far this is a fair picture of actual Greek democracies. Our knowledge, as far as any detail goes, is practically confined to Athens, and we therefore always tend to think of any criticism of democracy as applying mainly or entirely to her. Undoubtedly, if we think only of Athens, we should be inclined to feel that the picture was considerably overdrawn. But there are good reasons for thinking that Athens was an exceptionally favourable specimen of the class, and her constitution was certainly much more stable and securely based than the majority of Greek democracies. Plato himself was, like so many writers of his time, severely critical of the Athenian democracy, and the tendencies he dislikes undoubtedly made their appearance there to some degree from time to time. But he was well acquainted with the history of other Greek states, and it would be a mistake to think that he was necessarily thinking solely, or even mainly, of Athens. Some of the details he gives by way of illustration are hard to square with what we know of Athenian conditions, but they may well have appeared elsewhere. It is significant that in one of his letters he uses almost the exact phraseology of the *Republic* in criticism, not of Athens, but of the democracies in the Greek cities of Italy and Sicily. And the account of the eventual downfall of the democracy is certainly taken in most of its detail from the history of Syracuse. Altogether, it seems clear that Plato is not trying to give a detailed picture of any particular state or states, but rather a generalized account of what the tendencies that led to democracy would develop into if unchecked.

At any rate, it is from this internal conflict that the last and worst of the forms of government takes its rise, when a popular leader exploits the fears and suspicions of the democracy to secure the supreme power for himself, in the form of a tyranny or arbitrary dictatorship. This was, of course, a recurrent phenomenon in Greek political life. And for Plato, as indeed for most Greeks, it was the lowest stage to which a city could sink. Whereas every other form of government rests on some notion of good for a community, even if it is only the negative good of not being ruled by anyone, the tyranny is the direct negation of any notion of a good for the community, in that the community comes to be treated merely as a means for the satisfaction of the arbitrary desires of one man. It is not the mere fact of the power being in the hands of a single person that Plato finds so objectionable. If the single ruler is superior to anyone else in wisdom and devotion to the good of the whole community that may be an excellent form of government. But it is the essential feature of the typical Greek tyranny that it is the result of the selfish personal ambition of a completely un-scrupulous individual, who regards everyone else as merely the instruments of his own ends.

This, then, in outline is Plato's estimate of the actual types of government that he finds in the Greek cities. And, parallel to each of them, he also sets out corresponding types of character in individuals. In spite of some brilliant pieces of characterization this is not of major importance. But his general account of the different elements that make up indi-vidual character is of great interest. It is the most systematic description that he gives us of his view of the individual per-sonality, and, as far as we can judge, the view remains substan-tially the same throughout his writings. He starts with an analogy between the structure of a community and the structure of the individual personality. But he does not commit the fallacy of supposing that an analogy can provide a proof of anything. He uses it as a pointer to suggest a possible line of inquiry, and his conclusions are arrived at on the basis of an examination of each side of the analogy on its own merits. So he goes on to an examination of the individual personality to see whether we can find within it distinctions at all corresponding to the distinctions between the different classes or functional groups in a community.

One of the most familiar facts of human experience is the fact of mental conflict. We constantly find something in us which impels us in one direction and something else in us which holds us back from it. And that suggests that the human per-sonality, as we know it in this life, is not a single, uniform thing, but a complex of different, and sometimes opposing elements. That indicates the kind of analysis that Plato is attempting. It has, for instance, nothing in common with the familiar psycho-logical distinction between cognition, conation, and feeling. It is rather a classification of the main influences or impulses that affect our actions. And it is suggested that these can be classified most conveniently under three main heads. In the first place, there are the physical needs or desires. The most obvious of these are hunger, thirst, and the sexual impulse, though doubtless they would include other minor instances, such as the need for rest when fatigued. On quite a different level is the second class or element, which Plato describes by a word usually translated 'spirited'. It is, by the way, most desirable to avoid the use of the noun, 'spirit', in this connexion, because this obviously in some of its uses has suggestions in English which have no connexion whatever with the Greek word. In various passages he speaks of this element as that which leads us to defy danger or display courage, to be led by ambition and to desire power, prestige, and glory, to feel angry when we are wronged or thwarted, and ashamed or angry with ourselves when we have done wrong. At first sight this may seem rather a varied collection to bring under one head. But a little further reflection will show it as a sound piece of psychological observation. For, in fact, we can see for ourselves that all these types of behaviour have a common basis in the feeling for oneself, the impulse to self-assertion or the 'self-regarding instinct', as some psychologists like to call it. That is really what the 'spirited' element is.

The highest level is that of the rational or reasoning element in us. This is not, of course, merely the cognitive process, for it includes also the impulse or desire to use this process. Nor must we think of it as merely the desire for knowledge, though, of course, that is one side of it. We can best describe it, perhaps, as the desire or impulse to be rational, which, as applied to our conduct, leads us to try to get rid of inner contradictions and to harmonize our varying impulses into an ordered system of behaviour. And trying to do this involves trying to understand ourselves, our relations to our society, and finally our relation to the whole of reality and its ultimate principle, the Form of the Good. The desire to harmonize ourselves and the desire to know and understand are to be thought of as inseparable parts of the same process.

The ideal character, then, is a perfect harmony of these elements. In the nature of things the rational element must be the guiding and controlling principle. The 'spirited' element is regarded by Plato as the natural ally of the rational. We can see for ourselves, when we set out on some course which our reasoning tells us is right and find that we are faced with difficulties and unpleasantness and danger, how helpful it may be to call on our pride or self-respect, the feeling 'I am not going to be beaten by that', to strengthen our determination to overcome them. Yet obviously this feeling may on occasion be carried too far and may have to be checked by the reason. The physical desires, too, are in no sense in themselves bad. Indeed, their satisfaction is necessary for the preservation of our own lives and the continuation of the species. But it is bad when they come to be regarded as the chief aim and our reasoning powers are used merely as instruments for their satisfaction. All natural desires have a place in the good life. There is no suggestion here of the desirability of 'mortifying the flesh' or of self-denial for its own sake. But any particular desire may often have to be held in check, so that we may get the maximum satisfaction of, in Plato's phrase, 'what the soul wants'.

In the light of this, we can see in what sense, for Plato, virtue is identified with knowledge. Knowledge is the distinguishing mark of virtue. But it is not the whole of virtue. Complete virtue consists in the proper ordering and control of the various emotional tendencies by knowledge. These emotional tendencies are, so to speak, the raw material which the reason, in the light of its knowledge, works up into the finished article. But to do this reason has to have its own drive, 'the love and desire that go with it', as Plato says in the *Laws*. And, as we have already seen, he believes that the innate strength of this drive varies considerably between individuals, as does also the innate capacity for using the reason. We have seen, further, that the reasoning capacity cannot work properly unless the other emotional tendencies are to some degree ordered and controlled. So, if it is true that complete virtue is impossible without complete knowledge, it is also true that the attainment of knowledge is impossible unless there is already some degree of virtue.

This begins to look like a kind of vicious circle: we cannot attain virtue without knowledge and we cannot attain knowledge without virtue. And it would be a circle, if we considered the individual in isolation. But Plato clearly feels that, except possibly by an occasional 'divine accident', no one can attain the full degree of goodness, of which he is naturally capable, by his own unaided efforts. His potentialities need training and education for their development, and that can normally only come from someone else. In the existing inferior cities we could, probably, only hope to receive such influences from a single exceptional individual, such as Socrates, or a small group of like-minded people, such as could be found in the Academy. But, though that may be the best that we can do in existing circumstances, it can never be a real substitute for the well-organized city, in which education and guidance are provided by the laws, customs, and institutions which enforce the established standards of value of the community. This is really just as necessary for the highly gifted few as we have already seen it to be for the great mass of the ordinary people. So the account of the ideal character of a single individual is really only an abstraction, and it requires the account of the ideal community, not merely as an analogy, but as the essential condition of its fulfilment.

The modern reader will probably still demand some further clarification of Plato's view of the relation of the individual to the community. In particular, he will want to know how much, if any, truth there is in the assertion of some modern writers that Plato regarded the community as something which has an end or good of its own over and above the good, not only of this or that particular individual, but of all the individuals in it, and that he thought that this good had a superior claim to the good of the individuals. The issue had hardly been formulated in Plato's day in the terms with which we are familiar. But, on the whole, the answer must be that this criticism is not valid. There is no passage anywhere in which Plato speaks of the city as having a good or purpose of its own which is in any way different from the good of its individual members as a whole, or which could even conceivably be thought of as in opposition to it. On the contrary, at the very beginning of his analysis he describes the purpose for which the city comes into being as the satisfaction of the needs of the individuals. In a later passage he says that any characteristics we ascribe to a city as a whole can only come to it from the individuals in it. In the well-known passage at the beginning of Book IV he states that our object is, not to make any particular group in the city especially happy, but to give as much happiness as possible to the whole city. The opposition here is clearly between the happiness of a few individuals and the happiness of the whole lot. There is no hint or suggestion, here or elsewhere, that there is, or could be, such a thing as the happiness of a city which was distinct from the happiness of the individuals in it.

On the other hand, it is certainly true that he believed that the individual apart from a community was an imperfect and fragmentary being, a mere collection of potentialities which were only realized in a society. But this realization is still something that occurs in individuals, and there is no new element over and above this. There is more plausibility in another criticism which has been advanced to the effect that Plato makes morality too exclusively a matter of duty to the city community, and does not give a proper place to the relations between individuals nor to the preservation of personal standards which might make an individual at times ready to stand up against the standards of his community. There may be some truth in this, but it is easy to exaggerate it. The subject of the *Republic* is morality in social life and it would be out of place to dwell at length on questions of right conduct between individuals. But it would be absurd to suppose that Plato underrated this or that he thought that kindness and fairness and honesty between man and man was of no account. As for the other point, it is only in the limiting case of the perfect community that the morality of the state and the morality of the individual are identical. For the good man living in the imperfect state the duty of non-conformity is clear, and is asserted by Plato in language that might almost have been used by a Cynic or Stoic in a later age.

The *Republic,* like all the dialogues, is written with a limited purpose. And that purpose has been achieved when we have been shown the ideal for the individual character, as we know it in this life, the ideal organization of a community, and the right relation between the two. But in the end Plato makes it clear that this is not the whole story. Our understanding of individual and society alike is imperfect until we have seen them in relation to the whole of reality, and understood their purpose in the light of the ultimate purpose of all things. We shall see what can be said about this when we come to consider the final form of Plato's metaphysical and religious beliefs.

Before going on to this, however, a few words must be said about the contributions to political thought in the later dialogues, particularly the *Politicus* and the *Laws*. These are considerable in amount. Indeed, if we were to judge from the space allotted to them we should have to suppose that the main interest of Plato's later years was political. The greater part of this space, however, is given up to discussions of detail, which, interesting though they often are, do not raise questions of fundamental political theory. On this, his position remains substantially unchanged, though there are significant developments on some points.

The *Laws* is the longest and latest of all the dialogues. It is said to have been left unrevised at Plato's death. There are certainly signs of this, and, in addtion, there are indications at times of a loss of grip on the argument, which may be due to old age. None the less it is of great interest, but as it is, in the main, concerned with a detailed account of the particular laws and institutions of the state which he is planning, a lengthy discussion of it would be out of place here. It differs from the *Republic* in that the state described is not the absolute ideal. It is, probably, not even the closest approximation to this that could be attained if every possible condition was as favourable as it could be. It is perhaps best taken as an account of the best we could hope to get if, as the imaginary situation of the dialogue supposes, we were starting a new city with an ordinary collection of Greeks. It is not often safe, therefore, to draw any conclusions about a possible change in Plato's views. On some points, such as the communism of property and of family relationships, we are expressly told that the provisions of the *Republic* still represent the ideal, but are not regarded as practicable in these circumstances.

That is a modification which present-day opinion would probably regard as an improvement. On other points we may regret Plato's reversion to current Greek ideas. Slavery, for which there was no place in the *Republic*, reappears as an institution. A point, of which a great deal is made by modern critics of Plato, is the introduction of the death penalty for the public profession of atheism. Yet, much though we may disapprove of this, it would be a mistake to exaggerate either its extent or its novelty. It is nothing like a full-blown Inquisition, as it is sometimes called. And there is no doubt that, as it was, in Athens the teaching of atheism would be a criminal offence under the law against ἀσέβεια or impiety, even though this law might not often be invoked in practice. There are other matters in which we should probably note with satisfaction the retention of the provisions of the *Republic*. The close restriction of disparities of wealth remains. And we still see the same fine enthusiasm for education and the demand that the community should take its responsibilities seriously in this respect.

It is sometimes said that Plato's judgement of democracy becomes more favourable in these later writings. And there is a certain amount of truth in this. Unqualified democracy still remains the most ineffective form of government, 'capable of nothing great, either for good or evil', as we are told in the *Politicus*. But in the *Laws* the general principle is laid down that for a state to be well governed there must be a proper balance between authority and liberty, and one conclusion from this is that a certain element of democracy must be introduced into the government, and that on some points the decision must be taken by the whole body of citizens. It is true that the citizens in the state of the *Laws* are not allowed to practise the manual crafts, and, apparently, not necessarily required to cultivate their own farms for themselves. But that is advocated on its own merits, and it is not at all clear that it is put forward as a necessary condition for the application of the general principle. What is pretty clear is that, whether or not Plato's opinion of democracy was becoming more favourable, his opinion of oligarchy was becoming relatively less favourable. In the *Politicus* he says that a bad oligarchy is worse than the worst democracy. And in the *Laws* he says that the transition to a desirable form of government would be easier in a democracy than in an oligarchy, where it would be almost impossible. It would seem that he had come to feel that, while there was little to be said for democracy as a permanent form of government, there were possibilities of development in it which would not be found in an oligarchy.

But the most valuable contributions to the development of general political principles come from the *Politicus*. On two points in particular we find in that dialogue penetrating and illuminating discussions which are still of value at the present day.

In one of these passages there is an examination of the nature of the special knowledge appropriate to the statesman, the political or 'royal' art, as Plato calls it. This, while not in essence contradicting the *Republic*, certainly clarifies the subject further and removes possibilities of misunderstanding in the earlier dialogue. The particular point to receive attention here is the distinction between this art of the statesman, and the other kinds of special or technical knowledge which are also of service in the work of government. None of these special kinds of knowledge are themselves the art of ruling. They are necessary instruments in its hands, but must always remain under its control. One particular illustration used here is the art or science of generalship. If a war is once started, that is the kind of special knowledge that tells us how it could be waged most successfully. But that knowledge does not tell us whether the war ought to be started or not. That decision can only be entrusted to the possessor of the highest knowledge, the art of the statesman. The same idea is indicated, with less precision, in an earlier dialogue, the *Euthydemus*, so it was clearly in Plato's mind from the beginning. But it must be admitted that the distinction between the art of the ruler and the art of the general is not brought out clearly in the *Republic*.

The same applies to all the other specialisms. And a further point arises. Each of them will be practised by those whose special tastes and talents lie in that direction and therefore the danger will always arise that each group of specialists, if left to itself, will tend to push the claims of its own specialism too far. The control of the statesman is always, therefore, essential. And his art consists, not in acting himself, but in controlling the active or executive capacities, and in knowing when and in what circumstances to set them in motion and when to stop them. It is his art which 'has the capacity of supervision', and its function is, in Plato's metaphor, to weave together all the other arts into the finished product of the perfect state.

All this must be done, of course, in the light of a knowledge of the ideal community and the ideal life for its members. That remains the first essential for the true statesman. But we now have a clearer idea of the form that the practical knowledge, which is also necessary for the statesman, will take. It consists fundamentally in the knowledge of how to make use of the different specialized kinds of knowledge and skill. He cannot possess all these himself. But he must have the kind of understanding of them that is necessary to see how they can be used to contribute to the fulfilment of the ideal.

Another important application of this principle is to the judicial function, which even in the *Republic* is treated as merely one part of the duties of the rulers. Now we have the clear statement that the work of a judge is the work of a specialist with strictly limited functions. His business is to know and administer the law as it is, and he is not to concern himself with what it ought to be. This is an approach to the modern conception, which puts Plato clearly in advance of his age. To understand its further implications we must turn to the second point on which Plato's contribution is of outstanding interest.

This is the question of the nature, functions, and limitations of law as a guide to action in the community. And Plato's first point here is that, just because it is essentially a system of general rules, law cannot attain perfect justice or rightness in every case. For it involves treating a number of different cases as the same by ignoring their differences, whereas in fact no two cases are exactly alike, and we cannot tell beforehand what differences will be relevant. A perfectly wise and good man, therefore, would not act by general rules, but would think out each case as it arises and treat it on its merits. Such an attitude naturally has its appeal to thinkers who see the inadequacy of general rules for understanding any concrete situation, and to practical men, anxious to get things done, who feel their cramping effect.

But Plato also sees the dangers of this point of view. For we must always remember that, in fact, the actual people who will be called on to adopt it in practice are, as a rule, very far from being perfectly wise and good. The claim to be free from the guidance of laws or general rules does, indeed, imply a claim to something approaching perfect knowledge and wisdom, at any rate in reference to the particular point in question. And that is a claim not to be lightly made or lightly accepted. For the vast majority of people, whether in political authority or private life, it is wiser and safer to follow strictly the guidance of the laws and not to try to correct their application in particular cases by executive action. That does not mean that our laws are immutable. But they are only established or altered after careful thought and discussion, and so represent the considered opinion of the people concerned much more truly than immediate action which is open to the influence of all sorts of irrelevant prejudices. Therefore, unless we are absolutely sure that we have, or our rulers have, perfect scientific knowledge of right and wrong, we shall do more for the wise government of the state if we insist on strictly following the laws, once they have been laid down, than if we try to deal with each case on its own merits. All this is an admirable statement of the case for the rule of law as against 'reasons of state'. *Salus populi suprema lex* as an abstract general principle seems unassailable. But in practice there are so few individuals really capable of applying it that attempts to do so would be likely to injure the welfare of the people rather than to advance it.

All this is discussed by Plato purely in its application to law in the strict sense. But we can see for ourselves how the same arguments could be applied, with the necessary modifications, to the conventional codes of conduct current in our particular society. For these normally take the form of general rules, though usually more flexible and less definite than a code of laws. The whole question of the value of general rules as a guide to action is a perennial subject of discussion among moral philosophers. And Plato's argument here provides a contribution to it that is worthy of the most careful consideration.

6

Later Developments: the Theory of the Soul

WHEN WE come to the later developments of Plato's general philosophical position we find that the obscurity of the evidence and the difference of opinion about its interpretation are greatly increased. On certain broad principles there is a fairly wide measure of agreement. But on most questions of detail, and even on some of the general principles, it would hardly be possible to say anything that would not be disputed by some authorities at the present day. There are various reasons for this. But one, in particular, deserves mention. It is fairly clear that, as time went on, Plato's theories had become the centre of lively discussion and criticism in philosophical circles in many quarters. And most of the later writings which deal with metaphysical questions have some current controversy of this nature in mind. They are directed, therefore, less to the general educated public and more to those specially interested in philosophical questions than the earlier dialogues. Further, except for the references in Plato and a few allusions elsewhere, we know practically nothing of all the philosophical discussions which were evidently going on at that time. A lot that is obscure in Plato would become much clearer if we could read the writings or listen to the arguments which provided the stimulus for the discussions in the particular dialogues. It is more than ever necessary, therefore, in reading these dialogues to recall our previous warning and not to read Plato as if he was writing to give a systematic account of his philosophy to us today. He is not writing for us, but for his contemporaries, and he is not giving a systematic account of his philosophy, but discussing controversies on particular points that had arisen in connexion with it.

It would be beyond the scope of this work to attempt an examination in any detail of the critical problems that arise in connexion with the interpretation of particular dialogues. But a partial, and very brief, exception may be made for one dialogue which has been to a special degree a subject of controversy in modern times. That is the *Parmenides*. The first part of this dialogue consists of an account of a scene in which Socrates, as a very young man, meets the aged Parmenides, and hears from him a series of criticisms of the Theory of Forms, which is represented as already developed. Most of the criticisms are directed, not so much against the existence of the Forms as against the difficulties which are found in the account of the relation between them and the particular sensible objects. This is followed by a second and much longer section in which we are given a series of arguments, put into the mouth of Parmenides, purporting to show the results that follow if we assert or if we deny the One, and equally if we assert or if we deny the 'Others', presumably the many particular objects. This is an extraordinary piece of highly formalized dialectical argument, in a style quite unlike anything that we find anywhere else in Plato's writings. Some of the arguments seem to most people clearly sophistical, and the dialogue ends abruptly with what has been called the 'portentous conclusion' that 'both the One and the Others, in relation to themselves and to each other, both are and are not, and appear and do not appear'.

Almost every conceivable interpretation has been given of the purpose of the dialogue, and divergent views have been put forward about almost every detail in it. It would be out of place to attempt to indicate these here, except on one point. Most modern commentators, though not all, consider it probable that the criticisms of the Theory of Forms put into the mouth of Parmenides in the first part of the dialogue represent criticism of Plato's doctrine which in actual fact had been made by his contemporaries of the Megarian school. This was the school that carried on, in Plato's day, the teaching of Parmenides and the Eleatics to the effect that reality was one, and that all diversity, change, and motion were unintelligible and therefore unreal. We have evidence that Plato had close contacts with the members of this school and it is very likely that they would make their contribution to the current discussions of his doctrines. But when we ask how seriously Plato took these criticisms a marked division of opinion appears. On the one hand, there are those who consider that he took them very seriously, so much so that he modified his doctrine in important respects to meet them. And most of those who take this view would be inclined to add that the direction in which the modifications were to be made is indicated, somewhat obscurely it is admitted, in the second part of the dialogue. If that is so, a full treatment of the Parmenides is essential for an understanding of the development of Plato's thought.

As against this, there are others, among whom the author of this volume must be included, who take an entirely different view. They would hold that Plato did not take these criticisms very seriously or at any rate that he did not consider them at all valid, and that he certainly did not modify his theories to meet them. In support of this view it might well be argued that the criticisms do not, in fact, deserve to be taken seriously, that they are, in the main, purely verbal and at most point to the need for the development of a more satisfactory terminology. As for the significance of the second part of the dialogue, it is noteworthy that of those who claim to find positive conclusions in it hardly any two agree as to what these conclusions are. It seems much more plausible to regard this second part as a reply to the criticisms in the form of a counter-attack. It is an imitation or parody of the dialectical methods of the Eleatics and Megarians applied to their own favourite doctrine that reality is one, and it shows that the rigid application of these methods can lead to impossible conclusions which would be particularly unwelcome to these schools of thought.

There are doubtless difficulties of detail in this interpretation. But they are much less than those which face any alternative view. It is certainly just the sort of purpose for which Plato would have used a dialogue, whereas, if the suggestions previously made on the point are accepted, it is very unlikely that he would have used a dialogue to announce an important change in his own view. Apart from that, to argue the case fully would involve a prolonged examination of details. But one more general consideration may be mentioned, which to some of us will seem fairly decisive. It is, in fact, quite impossible to find in Plato's later writings any sign of any modification of his main doctrine which could plausibly be ascribed to the effect of the criticisms in the *Parmenides*. There are certain modifications and developments, as we shall shortly see. But they are not in any of the directions that these criticisms might point to. The difficulties raised in the *Parmenides* are in the main concerned with the nature of the relation between the Forms and the particular sensible objects, and criticism is directed against the phrases, such as 'participation', 'presence to', 'imitation', and the like, which Plato had used to express this relation. On this point there is no evidence at all that Plato ever changed his view, and he certainly continued to use the criticized terminology as freely as if the criticisms had never been made. And this in itself seems sufficient warrant for the view adopted here that the *Parmenides* does not mark a turning-point in the development of Plato's views, and that its importance for tracing this development has too often been greatly exaggerated.

This may seem an inordinate amount of space to devote to saying that I am going to say nothing about the *Parmenides*. But in view of the importance that has been attached to this dialogue by many commentators it seemed impossible to pass it over in silence here. We may turn, then, to the developments and modifications which we can actually find in Plato's views. These must be looked for, in the main, in his latest writings. But we cannot altogether ignore the statements that we find in Aristotle, who was a student under Plato in the Academy for twenty years. This evidence has to be used with care. A good deal of it is very obscure, and it is not always clear whether the references are to Plato's own views, or to the views developed by his followers in the Academy. Further, Aristotle is not a very sympathetic or understanding interpreter of other people's opinions, and there are good grounds for criticizing his account of Plato in some passages. None the less, it would be absurd to dismiss his evidence altogether, and it can at least serve to supplement and explain what we can find in the dialogues.

We can distinguish two main directions in which Plato's thought was developing in his later years. In neither of them does he substantially alter the main results of his earlier speculations. The further developments are built up on a secure foundation of results already reached. But, while not incompatible with the general lines of what has been said before, they take us a good way beyond it, and this does involve certain modifications in detail. In the one direction, we find important developments in his account of the nature of the Forms themselves. With this we shall deal later. In the other, he seems to have been concerned, not with the problem raised in the *Parmenides* of the general nature of the relation between Forms and sensible objects, but with the problem of how this relation comes into being in any particular case. Why does a particular object participate in a certain Form? Why, indeed, does it come into existence at all? And, having acquired a certain character by participation in a particular Form, how does it ever come to change and to participate in a different Form or even cease to exist altogether? It is this problem of 'becoming', of creation and destruction, of change and motion, that particularly exercised Plato's mind in these later years.

The Forms, of course, are the principles of permanence and stability. And in the earlier dialogues he is chiefly concerned to emphasize that sensible objects can only be the objects of rational judgements and can, indeed, only be regarded as real at all in so far as they have themselves a relative degree of permanence and stability through their approximation to the Forms. But the Forms, as the principles of permanence, cannot explain why the sensible world changes. Yet it does. And Plato is no longer content, if indeed he ever was, to leave this unexplained as just something inherent in the nature of sensible objects, a sign and result of their imperfection and unreality. He now looks for a definite explanation of this, and he finds it in the presence and activity in them of Soul or Mind. This now appears as the cause or principle of change and activity over against the Forms which are the principles of permanence, and both are declared to be equally essential elements in reality.

There are hints of this earlier, as in the *Phaedo*, where he says that the most completely satisfying explanation of events occurring would be an explanation in terms of some purpose. But this is not followed up there, and for the full development of the idea we have to look to the latest dialogues, the *Sophist,* the *Philebus,* the *Timaeus,* and the *Laws.* Before considering this, however, we must retrace our steps and see what is said about the soul in the earlier works.

The word 'soul' is the usual translation of the Greek ψυχή (*psyche*). And if we must have a single word for this purpose, that is probably the best that we can find. But it may often be somewhat misleading. For us, with our inheritance of Christian ideas, the English word naturally suggests a substantial entity distinguishable from the body, and very likely surviving the death of the body. Now, there were plenty of Greeks, Plato at this stage among them, who believed that the ψυχή was, in fact, such a substantial entity and did survive the death of the body. But that is certainly not implied in the very use of the word. Without going too far back into original derivations, it will suffice to say that the first clearly recognizable use of the word in Greek literature is to indicate that, whatever it is, which distinguishes a living being from a dead or inanimate object. In some passages, even as late as Plato or later, it can only be intelligibly translated as 'life'. This vital principle is found, of course, in all living creatures, and Aristotle can speak without noticeable incongruity of the ψυχαί of plants. But, in fact, the word is very rarely used except of human beings, and to a Greek it would probably in the first place suggest everything in a human being which made him more than a piece of matter. Here again the word by itself would not necessarily imply any view of this as a separate or distinguishable entity which could conceivably exist apart from the body. Thus, Plato himself, in the passage discussed in the preceding chapter, attempts an analysis of the different elements that we can discover in the human personality, and speaks of them as the different elements in the ψυχή. Here there is no reference to the soul apart from the body: indeed in a later passage, which we shall consider shortly, he hints at a doubt whether the soul, after it had been freed from the body by death, would in fact display these different elements. He is conducting a psychological investigation into the elements in human nature as we know it in this life, and there is no reference to anything beyond. In passages such as this the more neutral word 'mind' would probably convey the meaning better than 'soul', though even that is not perfect as a translation. For it is sometimes used with special reference to the thinking aspect of mental activity, and so is useful as a translation of the Greek word νοῦς (nous). But enough has been said to indicate the kind of implications that the word ψυχή had.

The word in itself, then, is non-committal, and its use is compatible with the widest divergence of views about the nature of this vital principle, and in particular its relation to the material body. To Homer, for instance, the soul after death survives apart from the body, but only as a shadowy wraith, one of 'the strengthless heads of the dead', deprived of everything that made life in the body worth living. And no doubt many people in Plato's day, brought up as they were on the Homeric poems, still held much the same view. Many others would not have allowed even this degree of immortality, which in any case cannot have meant very much to anyone. To them the 'soul' only existed in combination with the body, and death meant, in the words that Plato makes Socrates use in the *Apology*, 'to be, as it were, nothing and to have no perception of anything'. But there was also another view, sharply contrasted with these, which regarded the soul, as distinct from the body, as the real personality, and held that as such it survives bodily death. Indeed, it does not, on this view, attain its fullest and richest life until it is freed from the trammels of the body. With such a view was generally combined the notion that what happens to the soul after death is determined or affected in some degree by what it does in this life. Such beliefs, as we might expect, seem to have been specially associated with certain religious movements, particularly those known under the general title of Orphism, and also with the philosophical schools of thought which followed or were influenced by the teaching of Pythagoras.

Socrates probably, and Plato certainly, were much influenced by these views, though we need not suppose that either adopted them in the exact form put forward by any particular school of thought. In Plato's writings they first appear in the *Gorgias* and the *Meno,* but in neither is any attempt made at a proof of them. In both, the views are put forward in the first place for the light they might throw on some other problem. In the *Gorgias* it is their ethical bearing which is in question, and in the *Meno* they are put forward as a tentative hypothesis to explain some difficulties in the theory of knowledge. It is not until we come to the *Phaedo* that we get a systematic attempt to establish the immortality of the soul by rational argument.

In this famous dialogue Socrates, on the day of his execution, is asked to justify the serene confidence with which he faces his death, and in reply proceeds to develop the grounds for his belief, which apparently comes as a novel surprise to his friends, that the soul survives death and that to be freed from the body, so far from being an evil, is a release from evils and an entry into a better state. There is a long discussion and many arguments are brought forward, all converging on the same conclusion. Some of these arguments depend on ideas peculiar to that age and would make little appeal to us now. But others, though their form may seem somewhat unfamiliar, are in substance very much the kind of argument that would have to be used in our own or any other age to justify a belief in human immortality.

It would take too much space to consider these arguments in detail here. They rest, in general, on the belief, which seemed to Plato to be confirmed by a proper analysis of the facts, that there is a great deal in human life and experience which cannot be explained by physical and bodily processes. There is, for instance, our moral experience, which seems to assume that we can at times set ourselves in direct opposition to what the body asks for. Even when not in opposition the moral claim is something very different from the fulfilment of bodily needs. In another direction the facts of rational knowledge show that it is something much more than sense-perception, and that the most important elements in it cannot be explained by physiological processes at all. This is very much the line of argument followed by a modern defender of the separate existence of a soul, Dr. William McDougall in his *Body and Mind*. There we read, 'Consciousness of value, like consciousness of meaning, is a mode of consciousness which has no counterpart in the physical sphere: value, like meaning, is a purely psychical fact.' Again, it is argued that destruction and dissolution, as we know them, imply a process of separation of physical elements, and that we cannot intelligibly think of that as applying to a non-physical object. Finally, we get the argument that whatever it is which brings life to a non-living body cannot itself cease to live.

In the *Republic* we get a further argument which may be regarded as a special form of the general argument, already mentioned, that the modes of destruction by which physical objects that we know to be perishable are destroyed do not appear to be applicable to the soul. The special form of this argument here can hardly be made even plausible to a modern reader. But it is unnecessary to point out the flaws in it. What is of more interest is to note the bearing of this point on the general subject of the dialogue. It is introduced as a sort of appendix at the end, and gives an added force to the demonstration that the good life is preferable to an evil one. But it can hardly be said that it is an essential part of this demonstration. It seems clear that Plato would have held that, apart altogether from the question of personal immortality, a proper understanding of ourselves as we are in this life would give adequate grounds for this conviction. It is to be noted that the other characters in the dialogue accept the argument in favour of the good life as convincing before they have been introduced to the idea of immortality of the soul, an idea which is represented, as it was in the *Phaedo*, as coming to them as something of a surprise. It is possible that Plato at this stage of his thought held, as Kant did, that a proper development of the implications of our moral judgements would point to a belief in immortality. But, again like Kant, he would certainly have said that the conviction of the validity of our moral beliefs must come first and provide the basis for the further conclusion.

There is one other point, of even greater importance, in the argument in the *Republic*. At the end of it Plato refers briefly to its bearing on the tripartite analysis of the soul or human personality which we have previously considered. This analysis, he tells us, only applies to the soul as it appears in this life. It is hard to believe that it could apply to the immortal soul as it would be in itself apart from the body. If we want to know what this would be like we must look at the highest element, the reasoning element in us. It is this alone, he clearly implies, which survives death, and the other elements are merely ways in which the soul acts when associated with the body in our life on this earth. The conclusion seems to follow inescapably that soul in itself is good, for it would be a contradiction in terms to speak of the rational element in us as evil, and that it can only be infected with evil by its association with the body. This is quite incompatible with the other possible view that the immortal soul by itself can acquire a particular character in the course of its life here on earth, so that some souls may be good and some bad, even after they are freed from the body. This latter view is more familiar to us, and it also appears in Plato. The contradiction between the two is never explicitly resolved. But it may be noted that the latter view appears, in the main, when Plato is speaking in the language of myth and poetry, whereas in his reasoned argument he generally inclines towards the former.

So far as this represents Plato's view, we can see in a fresh light what must have been the true significance of the belief in immortality for the final development of his moral beliefs. For him, as for later religious writers, the urge to goodness was ultimately the urge to 'lay hold on eternal life'. But that does not mean that we should act with a view to what may happen to us or what we may become in some future state. It means rather that we should act so as to give the fullest play here and now to that element in us which is immortal and therefore truly real. We shall see, as we go on, reason to believe that Plato's firmest beliefs tended more and more in this direction.

In the *Phaedrus,* which was probably written a little later than the *Republic,* we get a new approach to the question. The argument is now based on the fact of motion. Inanimate objects only move if motion is imparted to them by some force from outside. Anything that can move itself on its own initiative we regard as animate, that is as having a 'soul' in the Greek sense. This power of moving itself is, indeed, in Plato's words 'the

essence and definition' (οὐσία καὶ λόγος) of soul. The originat-
ing principle of motion must be eternal, otherwise all motion
would eventually cease. So every soul is immortal.

As it stands, this argument does not make much appeal to
us nowadays. It depends on the assumption that material objects by themselves always tend to a state of rest and that the fact
of motion calls for special explanation, beyond the nature of
matter. This idea was widely, though not universally, held by
Greek thinkers, and in the state of knowledge of the time was
a not unreasonable generalization from experience. But in the
course of the development of the modern scientific outlook
it has long since been abandoned. It is, however, of more importance for our present purpose to note the change of emphasis that this involves for Plato's thought. In the previous
arguments, in the main, the interest lies in what we can discover
in our own personal experience, in, for instance, the experience
of moral conflict or the attainment of scientific knowledge. But
now the interest becomes wider and extends to the characteristics of the world about us. We consider the general nature and
conditions of motion, which is a fact that we observe in the external world just as much as, or more than, we experience it
in ourselves. The centre of interest, in fact, is shifting from the
individual personality to reality as a whole, and Plato is becoming more concerned with Soul than with souls.

This becomes clearer still when we turn to the dialogues of
the final period. In four of these there is some discussion of the
place of Soul in reality, and the general position is the same
in all, that Soul is the principle of activity and change and
movement and as such is just as much an ultimate element in
reality as the principles of permanence, the Forms. This does
not, of course, imply any departure from the fundamental doctrine that things which change and decay, which come into
being and go out of existence, are not fully real. For Soul, which
is the cause of change in physical objects, does not itself change
in the sense in which they do. It does not, that is to say, increase
or diminish or combine or separate or come into being or go
out of existence. It is true that, in a sense, it 'moves' or is active,
and Plato gives us some hints, into the details of which we need
not go, of the kind of activity which can be characteristic of an

eternal object. But it is itself uncreated and indestructible, and is therefore on a quite different level of reality from the created and destructible physical objects in which it works.

We get the first clear statement of this function of Soul in the *Philebus,* though, as so often in the dialogues, it is only brought in as incidental to the main subject of discussion, the psychological analysis and ethical evaluation of the different forms of pleasure. What we are told here is that we must suppose a cause of things happening in the physical universe, of their coming to be what they are, and of the process of change and motion. This cause must be found in the Soul, which works throughout the physical universe, so that we must come to think of this latter as an animate being. And there is a further point raised here. Not only do we find this process of change going on, but we also find that it takes place with a certain uniformity or regularity, which can be expressed in exact laws or formulae. So that we must suppose not only that there is a soul at work, but also that it is a rational soul or a mind ($\nu o\hat{v}s$). These two functions of Soul, as the cause of there being motion and change at all, and also as the cause of its orderliness and regularity, may not seem to be necessarily connected. Some later commentators, indeed, felt this difficulty, and went so far as to regard Soul and Mind as two distinct entities. This interpretation was not generally accepted in antiquity, and it would certainly be impossible to find any warrant for it in this passage. So far as Plato does distinguish here between Soul and Mind it is only in the sense that Mind or reasoning is regarded as one of the functions or forms of activity of Soul. And the most natural impression that we get from the later discussions is that he believed it to be its most essential form of activity, that in which the soul is most truly itself.

One more point remains for consideration. What does Plato now think of the individual soul and its immortality? No mention is made of this here, and that in itself may have some significance. For the main subject of the dialogue is the nature of pleasure and the relative values of the different forms of pleasure. And, as pleasure is essentially an experience of individuals, one might have thought that the immortality or otherwise of the individual soul would have some bearing on these questions. The only mention, however, of our individual souls comes in quite a different connexion. We are told that, just as the material elements out of which our bodies are composed come from the material elements of the whole physical universe, so our individual souls must come from the soul which animates this physical universe. If we are to carry this parallel further, we should have to say that, just as the material elements of our bodies will eventually dissolve and return to the material elements of the universe, so our individual souls will eventually return to the great soul of the universe. This is not stated in so many words by Plato here, but it is a possibility that is certainly suggested by his way of speaking. And there are certain phrases in the dialogues which we have next to consider which may seem to suggest it even more strongly.

The discussion in the *Philebus,* with which we have been dealing, is only part of a more general analysis of the different elements which make up 'everything that now is'. A detailed exegesis of this, and an examination of the problems that arise in its interpretation, would be impossible here. But it provides us with part of the evidence on which must be based any attempt to sum up the final phase of Plato's metaphysical doctrine. It is to this attempt that we must now turn.

7
The Final Metaphysic

ALL THE difficulties that we have previously faced are intensified when we try to sum up the final results of Plato's thinking about the nature of reality. Even in antiquity some of his doctrines were found obscure, and differences of opinion about their interpretation seem to have started among his immediate successors. We must expect, then, that differences of opinion at the present time should be just as marked. Indeed, we may well be surprised at the degree of agreement that in fact has been reached.

The situation is complicated rather than clarified by the fact that when we reach this period we are not entirely dependent upon the dialogues for our evidence. We have also the statements of Aristotle based, presumably, on Plato's teaching in the Academy. Something has already been said about the difficulty of interpreting these. We have also one or two very brief allusions to the views of other pupils of Plato, and these allusions, brief though they are, are enough to suggest that Aristotle's interpretations might not have been unanimously accepted on all points by the members of the Academy. If we want to be on the safe side we should probably be wise to use this evidence only so far as it can be combined into a consistent scheme with the evidence from the dialogues. For it is on this that we must in the main depend.

The important dialogues of this last period are the *Sophist, Politicus, Philebus, Timaeus,* and *Laws,* which were probably produced in that order. There is no reason to suppose that there was any important change of view over this period, so that it seems best to consider this group of dialogues as a whole, and, whenever it is at all possible, to interpret any one of them in the light of the others, at any rate as far as we are concerned with their contributions to the understanding of Plato's general philosophical position. This qualification is important. For, as always, each dialogue has its own special interest, and the references to the general position assumed are incidental to that. The *Sophist* is mainly concerned with questions of logical method, the *Politicus* with politics, the *Philebus* with psychology and ethics, and the *Laws* with principles and details of legislation. There remains the *Timaeus*. There, too, the greater part of the space is occupied by an account of the physical and physiological processes in the world of nature. But as a preliminary to this there is an attempt to give, in the peculiar style of this dialogue, a picture of the general structure of reality on a much larger scale than in the other dialogues. Indeed, the account of natural processes, which is in the main taken over by Plato from recognized authorities of his own time or earlier, seems to be introduced primarily for the purpose of showing how it could be fitted into this general picture. Later tradition, from the time of Plato's immediate successors down to the end of the Academy, is unanimous in regarding the *Timaeus* as a key dialogue for the understanding of Plato's philosophy. And for us, too, in our attempt to understand this final stage of his thought, the *Timaeus* must take the centre of the stage.

The special difficulty in the way of an interpretation of the dialogue lies in the manner of its presentation. The important parts for our purpose are recounted in poetical language in the form of a myth. This takes the form of an account of the creation of the material universe by the Artificer or δημιουργός (*dēmiourgos*) which is described as an actual event in time. Hardly anyone has supposed that the myth as a whole is to be taken literally. In particular any notion that Plato regarded the creation of the universe as an event which actually took place is decisively refuted by the internal evidence of the dialogue itself. What we must suppose that he is doing is what we have already seen him doing, with much less elaboration of poetic imagery, in the *Republic,* that is, presenting the result of an analysis in the form of an historical account. He is trying to get down to the ultimate elements which we must believe to be involved in the existence and working of the natural universe as we know it.

But this still leaves room for a wide measure of disagreement about the exact interpretation of the symbolism used. Does each detail in the poetic imagery indicate a corresponding distinction in the rational analysis? It would be very hard to believe that. On the other hand, there has undoubtedly been a tendency among some commentators to go to extremes in the other direction and explain away so much as picturesque imagery that they leave us finally with something that has hardly any resemblance to the original account at all. But exactly where to draw the line between these two extremes is a very hard matter to decide. We must be guided partly by the internal consistency of the whole picture that we are able to draw, and partly by its consistency with the evidence that we can get from the other dialogues of the period. Even so, there will remain plenty of room for uncertainty, and in a summary account of our general conclusions, which is all that can be attempted here, there is bound to be an appearance of arbitrariness on certain points.

If my interpretation is correct, there are, in Plato's view, three ultimate and irreducible elements in reality, with two of which we are already familiar. The third is introduced to us for the first time in the *Timaeus,* but, once we have made its acquaintance, we can see that it is clearly adumbrated earlier. It is from the interaction or the mutual relations of these three elements that the material universe, with all its processes, arises. How far, if at all, they are thought of as having any existence or activity outside these relations is a question on which we can only speculate. So far as there is any answer to it, it will emerge in the course of our exposition. But it is clear that they are separately conceivable by thought, that each exists, so to speak, in its own right, and that no one of them is created by or dependent for its reality on another.

1. We may begin by considering Soul. We have already been introduced to the notion of soul or mind as the principle of activity, change, and motion throughout the universe, the cause

of anything happening or of any events that take place. And this general idea certainly remains unchanged to the end. But when we try to get a somewhat more detailed picture of the way in which Plato thought about this, we run up against many perplexing problems of interpretation, particularly in dealing with the account in the *Timaeus*.

It has already been pointed out that the story of the Creation in that dialogue cannot be taken literally. It is described as an actual event in time. But we are subsequently told that Time only comes into existence with the created world. Further, this created world, while not eternal, i.e. independent of time, is everlasting, in the sense that it 'has been, is and will be throughout all time'. The physical world is conceived of as a continuous process of events or things happening, infinite in duration, and Time, the 'moving image of eternity' as Plato calls it, is the mode in which this process takes place. The 'creation', therefore, is not a particular event, but a continuous process going on throughout all time, and to speak of it as a creation is meant to indicate that it is the work of the mind or soul which is active throughout the physical universe. Or, to put it in another way, 'creation' is the general feature of each event in the continuous process, not a particular act applying to the whole.

This is a development of the idea we have already met in the *Philebus*. But if we took the symbolism of the *Timaeus* as corresponding in each detail to the structure of reality, we should have to introduce a further complication. For the Artificer is described, not only as constructing the physical body of the universe, but also as constructing its soul and 'weaving it in' to the body. We can certainly not take this as implying the idea of a literal creation of soul, which would be even more out of the question than a literal creation of the whole body of the universe. But, even accepting that, there still remains the difficulty of deciding whether the Artificer, who must certainly be a soul, is to be regarded as a being distinct from the Soul of the World, which he is described as constructing. This would seem rather like suggesting, in our modern theological terminology, that there must be two Gods, one transcendent and one immanent, the latter in some way dependent on the former. Such an idea, however, would raise insuperable difficulties.

It certainly could not be fitted into the interpretation suggested above. But more than that, it could not be worked out consistently with itself, nor with the evidence from the other dialogues. It seems inevitable that we must regard the Artificer and the World-Soul as identical. The distinction made between them in the story would, then, symbolize merely different aspects of the activity of soul in reality.

There is less difficulty in interpreting, on these lines, the further stages in the account. The World-Soul, as such, is not apparently assigned any further function. But the Artificer is described as creating subordinate gods, by constructing and animating the chief heavenly bodies, particularly the planets, including the earth, 'the first and oldest of the gods'. To these subordinate gods is assigned the duty of creating the particular living beings, such as ourselves. What this seems to mean is that the activity of soul in the physical universe brings into existence physically separate bodies, each of which, of course, is animate or has soul in it, and thus may be regarded as a relatively distinct individual. The first great differentiation of this kind is into the heavenly bodies, primarily the planets and the sun and moon. And within each planet, particularly in our earth, there is a further differentiation into the individual living beings in it. The heavenly bodies, it seems, are regarded as permanent, created, and therefore destructible in principle, but not in fact destroyed, whereas the individual living things are, of course, coming into being and going out of existence all the time. It is worth noting that this account certainly suggests that the separate individuality of the particular souls consists entirely in their inhabitancy of physically distinct bodies. But it would be impossible to discuss this point at length here. Something more may be said on it, particularly with reference to the relation between the individual human souls and the soul of the universe, when we come to deal with the more specifically religious aspect of Plato's doctrine.

We have here, then, one of the ultimate elements in reality, the soul which animates the physical universe and is responsible for the activity and movement in it. The two most distinctive characteristics of the activity of soul, when it is most fully itself, are, on the one hand, desire and purpose, and on the other understanding and reason. The processes of the physical universe, for which the soul in it is responsible, must therefore be thought of as inspired and guided by a rational purpose. We have only a few hints about the way in which this idea could be used to explain the reason for particular processes. But we shall understand the general direction of the purpose better when we come to consider the second fundamental element in reality.

2. This consists of the Forms. It is, perhaps, hardly necessary at this stage to enter on any lengthy exposition of the view that these two are separate and co-ordinate elements. The Forms are not souls, and Soul is not a Form, and neither is 'made' by or dependent for its existence on the other. This is quite clearly and unmistakably implied by Plato's general way of speaking of the two, and those who at various periods have attempted to reduce or subordinate the one to the other have generally had to come back in the end to one form or other of the argument that Plato must have meant that, because that is what they believe to be true. Nearly all scholars at the present time would recognize them as two distinct, irreducible elements in reality.

Plato's general way of speaking of the Forms in the *Timaeus* is very much the same as that which we find in the *Republic* and other earlier dialogues. We get the familiar contrast between the world of Being and the world of Becoming, 'the one apprehensible by intelligence with reasoning, remaining always the same, the other conjectured about by opinion together with unreasoning sensation, coming into being and going out of existence, but never actually being'. The relation between the two is described, again in terms that we have met before, as that of pattern to copy. In particular, the eternal realities, the Forms, are the model which the Artificer has before his eyes in framing the material universe, which he tries to make as like this model as it is capable of becoming. The rational soul that is at work in all processes of nature apprehends the eternal Forms and is striving to bring the world of change and becoming to as close an approximation to them as it can. This general idea, again, has nothing in it which is not completely consonant with the earlier account.

When, however, Plato comes to speak of the Forms more in detail there are certain changes and novelties. We hear nothing more of the Form of the Good, as the supreme principle of the intelligible world. But language is used which suggests one supreme Form, though it is not spoken of as distinct from or above the other Forms, but rather as containing them within itself. And this supreme Form is the model of which the whole physical Universe is the copy. The language used of it may seem, at first sight, puzzling and even misleading. For it is spoken of as the 'eternal Living Being' ($\zeta\hat{\omega}o\nu$), or the 'perfect ($\pi\alpha\nu\tau\epsilon\lambda\acute{\epsilon}s$) Living Being', or the 'Living Being which truly is', and it is said to contain within itself all the 'intelligible ($\nu o\eta\tau\acute{a}$) Living Beings'. To the reader unversed in the Platonic terminology this might seem to suggest that the Forms themselves were living beings, that is to say, that they had souls. The confusion, perhaps, would be easier in the English translation, because we are compelled to use two words, the adjective 'living' and the noun 'being', whereas the Greek only needs a single noun. In any case, it would be a complete mistake to think of the Forms in this way. A living being, in the ordinary sense, implies an animate body, which grows and moves and is active in all the ways in which the different kinds of living being are active. None of these things can be ascribed to a Form. But we can call the Form by the same name as the particular sensible objects, because they 'participate' in it. They have something in them which is an imperfect approximation to or 'copy' of the Form, and the soul in them is striving to develop this so as to come as close to the Form as possible. We shall see directly how much further we can go in filling in the details of the process as Plato conceived it. But for the moment we must be content with noting that the Forms of every kind of object found in the material universe are represented as in some way forming a whole or system, in which each of them has its place.

For further light on Plato's final view of the nature of the Forms we must turn to the evidence of Aristotle, about which something has already been said. There are sceptical critics who would disregard all this and maintain that Aristotle had merely misunderstood Plato. We cannot say that this is impossible.

There are undoubted misunderstandings in Aristotle of earlier philosophers, and also of certain passages in the Platonic dialogues. But it would clearly be foolish to dismiss his account too hastily until we have at least made some effort to see whether it can be fitted on to the rest of the evidence. The most important point for consideration is the assertion that, in the final stage of his thought, Plato identified the Forms with numbers. The doctrine is never explicitly asserted in the undoubtedly genuine dialogues, though it is a not unnatural development of some of the positions taken up in them. But it is unmistakably implied in the *Epinomis,* a brief appendix to the *Laws,* which may or may not be by Plato. On the whole, the balance of opinion in recent times seems to be in favour of its genuineness, but this cannot be accepted as certain. It might, in any case, be an expression of Plato's views, even if not actually by his hand. We are told little or nothing by Aristotle of the steps by which Plato arrived at this conclusion, and Aristotle himself seems in considerable doubt as to how it was worked out in detail. We ourselves, therefore, can do no more than make conjectures about the general considerations which might have led Plato in this direction, and we cannot even make conjectures about the detailed applications of the idea.

It is, perhaps, not very difficult to understand the kind of reasons that might have influenced Plato when he was thinking of the Forms primarily as the objects of scientific knowledge. Indeed, we have already seen indications of the view that the attempt to attain true scientific knowledge of the physical world involved the expression of it in mathematical terms. And, for Plato, to say that being expressible mathematically was the condition of being scientifically known would be the same thing as saying that it was the condition of being real. Historically, as already noted, Plato took over this general idea from Pythagoras and the Pythagoreans. They maintained that the only perfectly intelligible, and therefore the only perfectly real, aspect of things was their mathematical aspect, and they expressed this conclusion by saying flatly that 'things are numbers'. But, according to Plato, they made the mistake of thinking that the numbers, which constitute the intelligible reality, were to be found *in* the physical, sensible objects; and, if our records are to be believed, this certainly led them to crude, and even fantastic, applications of the idea in particular cases. For Plato, as we have seen, the sensible objects could never have the completely clear-cut and intelligible character of the objects of mathematical knowledge. They could only approximate to it. He would, therefore, correct the Pythagorean dictum, and instead of saying that things are numbers he would say that the Forms of things are numbers. This idea that the 'really real' world, that the scientist seeks to know, must be that which is expressible in mathematical terms is familiar to us in the writings of various scientific thinkers from the seventeenth century to the present day. Of course, the mathematical terms that the modern scientist has in mind would be something infinitely more complicated than anything Plato ever conceived of. But the general idea of scientific explanation is the same.

We can see, then, at any rate in a general way, what Plato was thinking about when he identified the Forms, as principles of scientific knowledge, with numbers. We shall be able to fill in a little more detail directly. But is it so easy to think of the Forms in that way when we are thinking of them as moral ideals? It might seem, at first sight, very difficult to imagine that in our endeavours towards the good we are really 'trying to be like' numbers. Yet it is not, perhaps, so difficult as it seems. For clearly numbers have, to a supreme degree, the property of perfect clarity and intelligibility, and also of permanence and independence of time, which for Plato were the primary marks of reality. And we have already seen how he might come to think of the striving towards perfection as a striving to attain full reality. Furthermore we constantly find specifically moral ideals spoken of in terms of a right amount of something, more particularly the right proportion between different elements. And this, at any rate in principle, ought to be capable of expression in numerical terms. So that it is not unnatural that the perfect Form of anything, towards which the imperfect particular instances are striving, should be regarded as finally expressible in a mathematical formula.

Before we leave the subject of the Forms, a word may be said on the particular problem of the kind of things of which Plato, in this latest stage of his thought, believed there were Forms. It is pretty clear, even from the dialogues, that he was no longer content with the simple view that whenever we gave a common name to a number of things we had to postulate a Form. In some of the later dialogues he has a good deal to say about this process of dividing things into classes and grouping them under a common name. And he makes it clear that the process can be carried out badly and things grouped together and given a common name which do not form a real class at all. For instance, in the *Politicus* he protests against the habit of classifying all the widely different non-Greek races, who have nothing in common except the negative fact of not being Greeks, under the head of 'barbarians'. A genuine classification must rest on a real distinction in nature. And it is only of such real classes that we can postulate Forms.

Aristotle has some incidental remarks on this point. He was possibly thinking of such a case as that just quoted when he tells us that the Platonists did not allow Forms of negatives. Mere absence of a particular property does not constitute a genuine class. Another fact of which he tells us incidentally is that Plato did not admit Forms of manufactured objects. This would certainly represent a change of view from the *Republic,* where we read of the Form of a bed, or rather of 'the Bed in Nature'. But it seems a reasonable modification. For the nature of a manufactured object depends purely on human purposes, and is alterable, within limits, at the arbitrary will of individual human beings. There cannot therefore be one fixed and unalterable numerical formula for it based on the nature of things, which can be the object of scientific knowledge. The general conclusion is summed up in the statement that, for Plato, there are Forms only of what exists in nature and forms a real natural kind.

There are other developments of which we get obscure hints, particularly the idea that the Forms or numbers themselves have an internal structure which can be analysed into distinct elements, with a relation between them corresponding to the relation between the Forms themselves and the material objects. But it would involve a disproportionate expenditure of space to discuss at a sufficient length to be intelligible the various conjectural interpretations of this doctrine that have been put forward. It remains, then, to deal with the third element which has to be assumed to account for the physical world.

3. It is made perfectly clear in the *Timaeus* that a third element in reality must be recognized. But exactly what part it is supposed to play has been a matter of controversy, and it must, indeed, be admitted that Plato himself uses phrases that are capable of being interpreted in diverse senses. It is only possible here to give what seems the most consistent and coherent interpretation.

It is undeniable that he sometimes speaks in terms which suggest the idea of a material out of which physical objects are made by the creative soul on the model of the Forms. This language must be to some degree metaphorical. We cannot think of it as literally a piece of physical matter nor of a literal moulding into the different forms that the particular objects take. He also speaks of it as something on which these different forms are imprinted. That, too, cannot be taken absolutely literally. Indeed, any attempt at a description must make a certain use of metaphor, for the exact terms which would indicate what he is trying to explain did not exist in the language. What is clear is that the objects in the physical world are not to be regarded as created out of nothing by the soul of the world. There is an independently existing element in reality, not created by anything else, and it is that which is capable of taking, through the action of soul, all the different forms of the material world, though it is itself without form. To speak of it as the matter out of which the physical world is made, or the receptacle on which the forms of physical objects are stamped, or the medium in which the soul works are all metaphors which help in one way or another to convey the meaning.

Plato is a little puzzled by the problem of the kind of knowledge that we can have of this. Obviously it is not an object of sense-perception. It can only be by a process of reasoning that we arrive at our conviction of its existence. On the other hand, it cannot be the object of rational scientific knowledge. As it is in itself formless, it is impossible to make any precise and definite statements about it. The best he can do here is to say that we know it by a kind of 'bastard reasoning'. But there is still something more to be said about it. We are not confined to describing it merely by negative terms. And he takes a further important step in the argument by identifying it with space. And we must consider briefly what he means by speaking of space as, in some sense, the matter out of which the material universe is made.

To the ordinary person the word 'space' suggests at first sight a vast emptiness. But it does not convey mere nothingness to us. For there is at least included in it some idea of position and direction, and from that can be developed the ideas of shape and size, in fact of all the qualities that we call spatial. But, of course, the general idea of space does not in itself include the idea of any particular spatial property, any one shape or size or position rather than another. Space is that which is differentiated into all the particular shapes and sizes that we know, but space itself is not any particular shape. The one essential fact about all material bodies is that they are spatial. If we take any particular material body we find that its particular spatial properties, its shape, size, position, etc., are constantly changing. But as long as it exists at all, it must remain in space and have some spatial properties.

That is a general and irreducible fact about all material bodies. It follows, further, that the essential feature about any particular kind of material body, which distinguishes it from other kinds of material body, is its particular spatial properties, which are ultimately a matter of geometrical form. We can only indicate briefly here how Plato worked that out in detail. Material bodies are all made up of the four elements, earth, air, fire and water, a traditional classification which Plato took over from earlier thinkers and which was widely accepted in his time. In different bodies these elements are combined in various ways and various proportions. But the elements in their turn differ from each other by being composed of minute particles differing in their geometrical shapes. And these geometrical shapes are again made up of different combinations of simpler geometrical figures. We need not linger further over the details of this account, or over the difficulties that have been found in it. But it is clear that for Plato the only qualities that belong to material objects in themselves, and to the stuff of which they were made, are the geometrical qualities. All other qualities are secondary, and, though there is no full discussion of this, they seem to be regarded as arising from the effect of the primary qualities on the sense-organs of the perceiving subject. The distinction between primary and secondary qualities, so familiar in subsequent speculation, had already appeared in the work of the Greek thinkers a generation or so before this. And Plato is here making use of it in his own way.

Something more remains to be said about the relations of this 'third form of being', space, to the other two. The different geometrical shapes that space takes are spoken of as 'coming into it and going out of it', and they are further described as 'the images of the eternally existing realities'. This seems to imply that when, for instance, a particular material object assumes a particular shape, say a triangle, the shape itself does not come into being but 'comes into' its object, as it were from outside. This makes us think, at first, in the light of what we have read in the earlier dialogues, of the Form of Triangle 'coming into' the particular object, and making it more or less triangular. But we now find that the geometrical shape, the triangle, which 'comes in' is not itself a Form, but is an 'image' of a Form, if we take, as we clearly must, the 'eternally existing realities' to mean the Forms. It looks, then, as if we must think of the triangle neither as a particular triangular object nor as a Form, but as something intermediate between the two. And there is other evidence which suggests that this is, in fact, just what Plato did think. For this is, at any rate, a plausible explanation of what Aristotle means when he tells us that, for Plato, besides the Forms and the particular sensible objects there were 'mathematical objects' intermediate between the two.

We must remember that in this final stage of Plato's thought the Forms are numbers. Now the figures with which the geometer deals are not numbers. But they are certainly not sensible objects. As we have previously seen, the propositions that the geometer proves about them with demonstrative certainty would not be absolutely true of any sensible objects. Why, then, should they not be regarded as Forms alongside the numbers? There are, I think, two main answers to this, the one expressly stated by Aristotle, the other to be inferred from the account in the *Timaeus*. In the first place, the geometer's propositions often deal with two or more of the same kind of figure. For instance, the proposition that two circles cannot touch one another at more than one point would not be literally true of any sensible circles that we could draw or make. It could only be true of mathematically perfect circles, which are grasped by the reason, but could not be perceived by the senses. On the other hand, there cannot obviously be two Forms of the Circle or two of the Circle Itself, touching one another. So there must be intelligible, non-sensible mathematical objects intermediate between the Forms and the sensible objects. In the second place, the geometer's figures still retain some element of space. And space is the essential feature of material sensible objects. So the trail of the sensible world still hangs about geometrical figures and they cannot be regarded as completely satisfactory objects of pure scientific knowledge. We only get away from the spatial altogether when we come to numbers.

This does not, of course, mean that there are not Forms of geometrical figures. But the Form of a geometrical figure is not itself a geometrical figure, but a number. The idea of the numerical expression of a geometrical figure was familiar in Greek thought before Plato's time, though for a variety of reasons the application of it did not get very far. Indeed, because of a defective arithmetical symbolism, the tendency in practice was rather in the other direction, towards the geometrical expression of numbers and their relations. But that was merely a practical expedient, and Plato would undoubtedly have been in accord with later mathematical ideas in holding that advancement in mathematical thought lay in the attempt to arithmetize geometry rather than to geometrize arithmetic. But we know little or nothing about the extent or the manner of his application of this idea in detail.

At any rate, so much is clear that the pure Form is a number or combination of numbers, and that the geometrical figure is a particular determination of space by numbers. We can see, in a general way, how the same would apply to the Forms of natural objects. We can speak, for instance, of the Form of Horse. But that is not a horse, an animal that runs about and kicks and is ridden. Scientifically, 'horse' in the first place implies a combination of different elements in a certain proportion which can, in theory, be expressed numerically. But these elements themselves are ultimately geometrical, and therefore, in the final analysis, also expressible in numerical terms. We cannot really go much further than that. It would be vain to attempt conjectures about the way in which Plato would have applied the general idea in detail, if, indeed, he ever attempted to do so at all.

There remains for consideration the bearing of this on the creative work of soul in the world. The actual forms that particular material objects take are the work of the soul in the world. But soul works in the medium of space, and it is clear that Plato thought of this as, in some way or degree, a limiting or resistant medium. The general spatial character of material objects is something that belongs to them independently of soul, though the particular character of particular objects is given them by soul. But what soul can do is limited by the general nature of space and the conditions that that imposes on the work of soul. Soul, as we might say, has not got an absolutely free hand, and its spatial limitations prevent it from bringing material objects to the complete perfection that it would desire in the light of its vision of the Forms. Theophrastus, Aristotle's successor who had himself been a pupil of Plato, sums up his account of Plato's views with the words, 'Wherefore not even God can bring all things to perfection but only within the limits of possibility.' The limitations imposed by the spatial character of material objects on what soul can make of them is described by Plato as Necessity $(\dot{\alpha}\nu\dot{\alpha}\gamma\kappa\eta)$, and the total result is to be thought of as a combination of the influence of soul or mind and 'Necessity'. The soul is always in its creative activity striving to overcome the limitations of the medium in which it works. It is trying, in Plato's metaphor, to 'persuade Necessity'. But it can never do this completely or absolutely, and there necessarily remains an irreducible element of imperfection in the material universe. We shall have something more to say about this in the next chapter.

8
Theology and Religion

PLATO'S THEOLOGY is, of course, part of his general metaphysical doctrine, and, as such, something has already been said about it. But the subject is of sufficient interest to warrant some degree of special attention, even at the risk of a certain amount of repetition. And we may begin by pointing out that Plato's primary and fundamental idea of God or the divine is of the soul or mind which he conceived as working throughout the physical universe in the manner described in the previous chapter. There are numerous passages in which he speaks of this as God, and the attempted proof of the existence of God or the gods given in the *Laws* is simply an elaboration of the general argument for the conception of soul as the cause of everything that happens in the universe, with which we are already familiar. This divine soul of the universe, as we have seen, contemplates the perfect Forms, and, using them as models, strives continuously to bring the physical universe to the greatest degree of perfection of which it is capable.

To the modern reader such an account will doubtless suggest many questions, most of which are much easier to ask than to answer. And this is largely due to the fact that the ordinary Greek's religious conceptions, from which the philosophers necessarily started, are so remote from ours, with our centuries of Christian tradition. We can probably, with some effort of the imagination, picture to ourselves fairly well the Greek's way of thinking about political or moral questions. But to reproduce in our minds the way he thought and felt about his gods seems almost impossible. Thus, if we were to ask, as we well might, whether Plato's God was a personal God, we should probably seem to ourselves to be asking a definite and intelligible question. Yet it is very doubtful whether Plato would have understood what we meant at all. For there was no tradition in Greek, as there is in Christian, thought which ascribed the concept of personality as an essential attribute to the godhead. Whether the notion of personality as ascribed to an Infinite Being is really so clear and intelligible as we are apt to assume may well be questioned. But at any rate we try to attach some meaning to it, whereas Greek thought hardly seems to feel the need of it at all. It is true, of course, that in the Homeric poems the gods are presented as having well-marked individual personalities. But that is only achieved by reducing them very near to the human level and picturing them as individual beings with 'bodies, parts and passions' like our own. It seems pretty clear that, at any rate in the period we know best, the ordinary Greek did not in fact habitually think of them at all like that. As far as we can judge, his fundamental notion was rather of vaguely conceived forces which could manifest themselves in a variety of different forms without being restricted to any particular one of them. It may be because he started from such an attitude that Plato, like, I suspect, most thoughtful Greeks, so often seems to us much more concerned about the general nature of the divine or the general attributes of divinity than about any question of the particular being or beings in which such attributes are found. The opposition between monotheism and polytheism, which was of such cardinal importance to Christian thought, rarely or never seems to have much significance for Greek thinkers, and Plato speaks indiscriminately of God or the gods when he is referring in general terms to the divine element in the universe. If we were forced, then, to give an answer to the question with which we began, we should probably have to say that God, in the sense of the soul of the universe, was not a personal being. He was, at any rate, not thought of as an individual personality alongside other individuals, but in some sense contained them all.

Towards the end of his life, if we can judge by the latest dialogues, particularly the *Timaeus* and the *Epinomis,* Plato did

arrive at much more definite notions about the particular forms
in which the divine soul manifested itself in the material universe. As we have already seen, he thought of this soul as forming and animating various material bodies, and among these
the first place is taken by the heavenly bodies, particularly the
sun, the moon, and the planets. In the details of his view there
are many difficulties and obscurities, and great opportunities
for differences of opinion in their interpretation. But the most
important point for our purpose is clear. These heavenly
bodies, according to Plato, can be shown, in spite of superficial
appearances, to move in a perfectly orderly and regular
fashion. And order and regularity are among the marks of the
ideal perfection to which God is always striving to bring the
material universe. Further, as we have already seen, they are
thought of as existing permanently throughout all time, whereas we human beings are continually coming into or going out
of existence. The heavenly bodies, then, represent the most
complete manifestation of the divine activity that we can find
in the visible world. And, if they are so regarded, it would seem
perfectly natural to Plato, or to any Greek, to speak of them
as gods, and to claim that they are appropriate objects of reverence and worship from the ordinary human beings, whose brief
existence and imperfect and disorderly behaviour are in such
striking contrast to theirs.

Were there, for Plato, any other beings which could be regarded in the same way? In the *Timaeus* he seems to hint that
we cannot rule out the possibility of the existence of some such
beings as the Olympic gods of Homer and the traditional
legends. But there is an unmistakable note of irony in the language that he uses of the popular beliefs about them. If, however, the *Epinomis* is a genuine work of Plato's, or represents
his opinions, we can go further. In that dialogue he not only
claims for the heavenly bodies that they are of a superior order
to us on the grounds already stated, but also that they are composed of different material elements from us, which is doubtless why they are capable of attaining such an infinitely greater
degree of perfection. And he goes on to suggest the existence
of other beings, composed of different elements still, which
occupy an intermediate place in the scale between us and the

heavenly bodies. That is to say that there is a hierarchy of super-
human beings, and all those of a higher order to ourselves are
proper objects of reverence and worship as divine. We are not
told much more in the way of detail about such beings, and in
any case we must always bear in mind the possibility that the
dialogue may, after all, not really be Plato's work.

We may still ask of these divine beings, the heavenly bodies
and the rest, whether, or in what sense, they are to be thought
of as personal gods, and still a satisfactory answer eludes us.
They are, of course, physically distinct bodies. But, apart from
that, nothing is said about them which would suggest what
we mean by distinct individual personalities. Probably the best
that we can say is what we have already said, that they are mani-
festations of the divine soul in physically distinct bodies. We
may, perhaps, note in passing how much the difficulty of trans-
lating these ideas into our own language is increased by the fact
that there is no indefinite article in Greek. We mean something
different by speaking of 'soul' or 'a soul'. But the Greek had
no way of expressing that difference, and perhaps, for that
reason, may not have been nearly so clearly aware of it. Similarly, when we come across the word $\theta\epsilon\acute{o}s$ in Plato, or elsewhere, we may often find it very difficult to decide whether to
translate it by 'God' (with or without a capital letter) or 'a god'.
Anyone who will examine the many passages in which the
words $\psi\upsilon\chi\acute{\eta}$ or $\theta\epsilon\acute{o}s$ appear and experiment first with one translation and then with another will soon become aware of the
difficulty.

To revert to the main argument, the general relation between
God, conceived of as the soul of the universe, and the other
fundamental elements in reality has already been indicated.
The Forms, as we have seen, are self-existent, not created by
or dependent on God or anything else. They are known by
God, who takes them as the standards of perfection towards
which He is striving to bring everything else. To the old question whether God wills the good because it is good, or whether
it is good because God wills it, Plato would have certainly re-
plied in the former sense. Indeed, in an earlier dialogue, the
Euthyphro, he does so reply in set terms, though, at that early
stage, we cannot tell how far it had yet become a settled con-

viction. Similarly, God is not a Form, though He is 'akin' to the Forms, in that, like them, He is immaterial and immortal, and also by His capacity to apprehend them and His desire to fashion the universe in which He works after their likeness.

His relation to the other irreducible element in reality, the spatial or material element out of which the physical world is made, calls for a little more discussion. We have already seen reasons to believe that this material element must be regarded as responsible for the evil in the world. Indeed, we find unmistakable statements in several passages in the latest dialogues to the effect that the cause of anything going wrong in the physical universe, or any part of it, is to be found in its bodily or material nature. And there are indications that this was the accepted interpretation of Plato's teaching among the writers of the generation that followed him.[1]

On the other hand, there is a passage in the *Laws* which has been sometimes taken to represent a different point of view. In this passage Plato argues that soul is responsible for everything that happens in the physical world, and, as both good and evil things happen, there must be more than one soul to account for this. There must be at least two, one responsible for the good that happens and one for the evil. This remark, which is here thrown out almost casually, has provided the foundation for a tremendous erection of theory by later commentators. In antiquity, Plutarch, and others who followed him, took it to imply a sort of Manichaean view of two world-souls, one good and the other evil, striving for mastery with each other. But there is certainly nothing of this in Plato. He does not, incidentally, even say that there must be two souls, but that there must be *at least* two, i.e. more than one. But some modern scholars, without going as far as this, have read great significance into the passage, and have suggested that by implication it is a denial of any view that would look to matter as the cause of evil. Yet if it is intended to mean that, it stands curiously alone among the relevant passages in Plato, and seems, indeed, in complete contradiction to other passages,

[1] See, e.g., *Politicus*, 273b: *Timaeus*, 86b: Aristotle, *Metaphysics*, 988a: Eudemus, in Plutarch, *De Animae Procreatione*, etc.

both in suggesting that soul itself can ever be anything but good and in denying that matter is in some sense the cause of evil.

Perhaps a solution of the difficulty may be found if we inquire further what constitutes a plurality of souls and what makes any particular soul evil. On the first point, it has already been suggested that what separates one soul from another is, in the final analysis, its inhabitancy of a physically distinct body. That certainly seems to provide all the plurality that the argument requires. On the second, it would seem, as we are expressly told in the *Timaeus,* that what makes any particular soul evil is the influence on it of the body with which it is conjoined. We only need, then, a slight modification of the original statement to bring the various passages into harmony. When we say that matter is the cause of evil that does not mean that matter is evil. Matter by itself is neither good nor evil. Nor does it mean that matter by itself is the sole and sufficient cause of the existence of evil. For any actual evil to exist or any evil action to be done there must be a soul at work. But what makes the soul do evil is its distortion from its true purpose by the influence of the body.

It must be admitted that, to a great extent, we are moving here in the realm of conjecture. That an evil soul becomes evil through its corruption by the body seems to be the consistent teaching of Plato, and we are certainly not told of any other way in which it could become evil. Further, it would seem a very natural conclusion to draw from this position that, if soul apart from the body is perfectly good, there cannot be a number of individual souls apart from the body. For it would not fit in at all well with Plato's general point of view to suppose that there can be a plurality of perfect beings. Indeed, quite apart from Plato, such a notion is very hard to think out clearly, if we are in earnest with the idea of perfection. We cannot, however, say with any confidence whether Plato finally arrived at this conclusion, nor, indeed, whether he asked himself the question in these terms at all. He clearly did not hold this view at the time, for instance, at which he was writing the *Republic.* But, as has already been suggested, the subsequent development of his doctrine would, at least, make such a view a natural and coherent part of it. And that is, probably, about as far as we can go.

There is one further point that calls for a brief mention. If such a view was held it would seem the logical conclusion from it that, when an individual body was dissolved by death, the soul that animated it would cease to exist as a separate individual being and would, in some way, return to the world-soul from which it originally came. There are certain phrases in the poetical language of the *Timaeus* which undoubtedly suggest that. On the other hand, there are passages in that dialogue which suggest the possibility that an individual soul might continue for a time in a separate existence by a process of reincarnation into another body. What exactly the point of identity would be between the successive lives is hard to see, and Plato says nothing to help us. In any case, even in these passages, this is not represented as the final goal. It is regarded rather as the punishment for an evil life, and the good soul is exempt from it. And we must always remember the possibility that, as some commentators in antiquity supposed, this whole account is merely allegory or poetic imagery and not intended literally at all.

Further speculation on these points would be profitless. But there is a good deal more that we can say about the relation that exists or ought to exist between God or the gods and the individual human beings as we know them in this life. And the first point to note is that Plato, in the *Laws,* insists that we must believe, not only that the gods exist, but also that they are not indifferent to human beings, but are concerned about them and their affairs. At first sight, this might suggest the Christian notion of the loving Father who cares for each of us individually as one of His children. But when Plato goes on to explain and defend his view we find little trace in it of such a notion. The emphasis is much rather on our usefulness as instruments in the furtherance of the divine purpose. All that we do and are makes some difference to the fulfilment of this purpose, and none of it therefore can be a matter of indifference to the divine soul whose purpose it is. There are some obscure hints, here and elsewhere, about the way in which God can fit us in to His purpose while at the same time leaving us a limited amount of freedom of choice between good and evil. But that is a point which does not seem to have worried Plato in the way in which it has worried so many Christian theologians.

So much for the relation from the side of God. What about our relation to Him? And here the first requisite in the right attitude of human beings towards the divine is right belief. We must believe firstly that God or the gods exist, secondly, that they are not indifferent to us, and thirdly, that they cannot be turned from their purpose by prayers or offerings or magical ceremonies. This last, of course, follows naturally. For if we believe that there is an active and rational purpose being worked out throughout the whole universe—and that is the essence of the belief in God—it would be absurd to suppose that that purpose could be changed for our convenience by any inducements that we could offer. These three doctrines must be accepted by all members of the society described in the *Laws,* and open denial of them is to be punished by imprisonment or death. But it does not appear that, once these fundamental beliefs are accepted, there is any compulsion to accept any particular view of the way in which they should be worked out in detail.

From what he says in the *Laws* and elsewhere it would seem clear that Plato believed that these doctrines were capable of rational proof, and that it is because of that that they must be accepted. And yet there have been some who doubted this, and it is worth while spending a little time in considering another view that has at times been put forward. This view would maintain that Plato was alive to the fact that there are certain truths, and these the highest of all, which are not accessible to scientific or philosophical reasoning, but can only be attained by some sort of direct religious experience or mystical vision. And it would suggest that Plato is trying to lead us to this when, in so many of the dialogues, he has recourse to the language of poetry and myth, and gives us an imaginative picture of, say, the creation of the world or the fate of the soul after death. Thus, by the 'fine frenzy' of the poet and the emotional and religious ecstasy that it arouses, we are led to a grasp of truths that reason cannot give, and which, as some have held, may even contradict the conclusions of reason. The great myths in the dialogue represent, therefore, Plato's attempt to carry us on beyond the limits that reasoning can reach to a higher level of knowledge.

Such a view as this will have its attractions for many. But for attributing it to Plato there are really no solid grounds at all. Everything that he himself says goes to show that for him myth and poetry were below, not above, reasoning. The only serious argument that those who would attribute a different view to him can bring is that he did, in fact, make use of myth in his dialogues. But to argue from that is to forget the clear and definite statements that he makes in his letters, to which we have already referred in an earlier chapter, that the highest results of philosophical reasoning cannot be conveyed in a dialogue or indeed in any written work at all. If the use of myth, therefore, indicates anything it indicates not the limitations of reason, but the limitations of its expression in a written dialogue. And the two are very far from being the same.

As far as the positive evidence goes there are several statements in different dialogues which indicate pretty clearly the kind of use to which Plato thought that myth and poetry could properly be put. In the passages in the *Republic* and the *Laws* which deal with the education of the young we have definite statements about the use to be made of myths and legends. They are regarded as a useful preliminary training by which our feelings and emotions are to be brought into the right state for beginning the serious business of intellectual study, and perhaps later as providing a kind of emotional reinforcement for our acceptance of the conclusions of this study. In other passages they are regarded as useful but inferior substitutes to be used for those whose minds are not sufficiently developed to grasp the highest truths of philosophy. Or again they may be used, as it were, as the expressions of a possible working hypothesis to guide our conduct when we have not yet attained true knowledge. But nowhere is there a clear suggestion that there is any alternative way of attaining this true knowledge except by the continued effort of hard intellectual reasoning.

There still remains one other possible explanation of the

introduction of the myths into the dialogues, which we must not forget. That is that Plato's chief reason for bringing them in was that he enjoyed doing so. It may be, though there is, of course, no proof of it, that the poet in Plato at times felt the need of a moment's relaxation from the strain of hard rational thinking and found it in the vivid imagery and moving language of the myths. Those who themselves are not fond of hard rational thinking may, if it pleases them, look on the poet in Plato as his highest self. But that would most emphatically not have been his own opinion. Indeed, he seems in general by our standards excessively harsh in his judgements of the value of imaginative literature. And it is important to remember, in reading these criticisms, that he is not a Philistine, depreciating what he does not understand, but rather one who was himself most fully conscious of the enchantment of words and therefore all the more alive to its possible dangers.

To return to the main argument, there is not much more that Plato tells us about the kind of knowledge that we can have of God or the divine element in the universe. It is noteworthy that when he is talking about the Forms he does at times, particularly in one or two dialogues, use language that might suggest that the final stage of our knowledge of them would take the form of a direct intuition rather than of a series of inferences. There is no suggestion that this represents an alternative way of arriving at knowledge to the discursive reason. It is rather the final stage of the reasoning process, and possibly a stage which can never be fully attained by individual human beings within the limits of this life in the body. But, in any case, he never speaks in this way of a possible knowledge of God or the soul of the universe. And that is, perhaps, only natural. For it is clear that for him we are in some sense parts of this soul, and our knowledge of the soul of which we are parts could hardly be on the same footing as our knowledge of the Forms, which always remain distinct from soul, as the objects which it knows. It is possible, as suggested above, that a complete knowledge, even of the Forms, could only be attained by the removal of our individual limitations, in other words, by ceasing to exist as separate individuals apart from the soul of the universe. This might seem to point to the ultimate ideal that we should *be* God and *know* the Forms. But that is going beyond anything that Plato actually says.

When we consider more in general his view of the nature of religious experience and the proper attitude of human beings to the divine, anyone brought up in the Christian tradition would probably, in the first place, be struck by one notable omission. There is practically nothing said about the need for any kind of direct personal relation between man and God, which is so prominent in most Christian teaching. This kind of purely religious experience does not seem to have occupied an important place, if any place at all, in Plato's thought. None the less the religious attitude, to which he does attach importance, is a very real thing. And it seems to contain two main elements.

In the first place we have to realize that each one of us is a small and insignificant part of the whole universe and that, as he says in the *Laws,* 'the parts exist for the sake of the whole, not the whole for the parts'. This sense of our own insignificance and the unimportance of our personal needs and desires is the first element in the religious attitude. But there is another side to it, which is of equal importance. For, though only small parts, we still are parts, and have our share in the working out of the purpose of the whole. Indeed, the purpose of the whole really is our purpose too. For, as we are told in the *Laws,* we suffer if we do not realize that the action which is best for the whole will also turn out best for ourselves, 'through the power of our common origin'. That is the second element in the religious attitude, the sense that by the conduct of our own lives we are taking part in a great enterprise, in which the soul throughout the whole universe is engaged. And we must keep alive the feeling of this in everything that we do.

How, then, does this attitude express itself? Primarily, and above all, in right conduct, the pursuit of virtue, and the avoidance of vice in our daily lives. The most complete expression of this is, of course, to be found in communal activity, co-operation in the realization and maintenance of a good community, when the possibility of that is open to us. The position here is substantially unchanged from that outlined in our discussion of the *Republic.* There is, perhaps, a stronger emphasis

on the insignificance of even the highest forms of political activity in comparison with the great cosmic process of the whole
universe. But that must never for a moment be taken to mean
that we need not be too serious about our own moral and
political conduct. On the contrary, as there is plenty of actual
religious experience to show, a sense of our own personal insignificance may be, and has often been, not only compatible
with but a powerful stimulus to the most strenuous endeavour
to realize a moral ideal in practice. For Plato, certainly, this
is the fundamental expression of the religious attitude as he
sees it. Indeed, from certain passages in the *Laws* we might get
the impression that the main value of holding true religious
views was as a means to the end of right conduct. That would
certainly be an exaggeration. The *Laws* is primarily a treatise
on questions of conduct, and therefore other considerations
are naturally treated from the point of view of their effect on
that. But it would not be an exaggeration to say that, for Plato,
religion is much less a form of activity distinct from morality
than a spirit in which morality is to be pursued.

This seems clearly implied in the latest dialogues. But there
are passages in some of the earlier writings, most noticeably
in the *Phaedo* and the *Gorgias,* in which a rather more other-
worldly point of view seems to be adopted. In reading these
we feel much more strongly the conviction that 'here we have
no abiding place', that death is a release from the evils of this
life, and that life, as we are told in the *Phaedo,* should properly
be treated as a preparation for death. It is quite possible that
there is a certain change of view, or at least a change of
emphasis here. But even if that is so, it is doubtful whether Plato
himself was fully conscious of it. There is a passage in the
Theaetetus which may express the transition between the two
views, or may equally express the true interpretation of the
earlier passages. There we read, in language reminiscent of the
Phaedo, that it is our duty to try to escape from this life to the
next—from Here to There, in the well-known Greek phrase.
But as we read on we find that this escape is not something for
which we have to wait till the end of our lives, nor something
that is to be achieved by withdrawing from the active pursuit
and practice of moral virtue in this life. 'To escape', he tells us,

'is to become as like God as possible: and we become like God by becoming righteous and holy and wise.'

So we may say that at all stages of his thought Plato believed that there was a sense in which we had to look beyond our life here on earth. But, certainly in the final phase and perhaps throughout, he did not suppose that this was to be achieved by thinking of it merely as a stage on the way to a better life in some future state. It was to be achieved by thinking of it as merely a small part of a great work which is going on here and now and for all time and everywhere. And that great work, the divine purpose, is not to get away from this material world, but to make it as good a world as it is capable of becoming.

In conclusion, a word may be said about forms of worship and religious observances. These play a large part in the life of a well-ordered community as described in the *Laws*, and what Plato has to say about them provides an interesting contrast with Christian ideas. From the Christian point of view, it would probably be true to say that the most important religious observance is the act of prayer. Yet about this Plato has comparatively little to say, and what mention he does make of it is in perfunctory and conventional terms. He has much more to say about religious festivals and sacrifices. The general tone of his references to these shows that he was thinking of them primarily as public acts of the whole community. Indeed, much the same seems to apply even to what he has to say about prayer. At times, at any rate, in speaking of prayer he seems to be thinking rather of what we should call hymns, written by the poets for the community. There is little or no reference to prayer as the approach of the individual soul to God. The general conception of religious observance as primarily a communal activity culminates in the provision laid down in the *Laws* forbidding all private religious observances and ceremonies. It must be remembered, however, that, at any rate, one important reason for this was strictly practical. The rule was laid down largely in order to protect individual citizens from being exploited by religious charlatans, who preyed on their superstition by pretending to have some special private magic of their own, which would secure the welfare of their devotees in this world or the next.

For the rest, it is worth noting that in the detailed provisions for public worship laid down in the *Laws* there is little or no trace of any special reverence being due to the heavenly bodies, which from the *Timaeus* and the *Epinomis,* and even from certain passages in the *Laws,* we had come to regard as the highest embodiments of the divine. On the contrary, the talk is all of the Olympian and other similar gods, and there is even an instruction to the founders of a new city to discover and keep alive the cult of any local deities specially connected with the place. This is a little peculiar, and it may possibly reflect a conviction that even such an important doctrine as this was not really fundamental and essential as compared with the general belief that there is a divine soul working throughout the universe, whatever particular forms it may take. That belief and the adoption of the right attitude of worship and reverence, of a sense of our own insignificance and submission to a purpose higher than our own, is the really essential element in religion. Any more detailed doctrines, and still more any forms or ceremonies, are of value primarily in so far as they produce and express this attitude. And, for the sake of public order and the sense of solidarity with our community, we had better adopt those which the customs of our own city or region dictate.[1] In an earlier dialogue, the *Cratylus,* there is an interesting passage which may have a bearing on this. Plato is there speaking particularly of the names of the gods, but the principle is obviously capable of more general application. In that dialogue he makes Socrates say that we really know nothing about the gods, either about their names or about themselves. Therefore in our worship we can call on them and pray to them as our own customs dictate. For we know no other way.

---

[1] There are also several references to the desirability of calling on the Delphic Oracle for instruction about the proper ordering of religious observances. But there is nothing incompatible in this with what is said above. For, from all that we know of the actual responses of the Oracle to such requests, it seems clear that its normal and regular instructions were to follow the laws of the city or ancestral customs.

9
Other Problems

THERE ARE a number of other questions, of interest to philosophers, on which Plato has something to say. Some of them are discussed in direct connexion with his general doctrines. But some he seems to have approached independently on their own merits. At any rate, his discussions of them can be considered, up to a point, without reference to the rest of his philosophy, though doubtless in the long run he would have tried to bring them into connexion. Many of these obviously have reference to current controversies, about which we are often very imperfectly informed, and they all clearly imply a background of thought and discussion which would have been much more familiar to Plato's readers than to us. There are tantalizing indications of the general views, both of Plato and his contemporaries, on many points about which we can only make uncertain conjectures. It would be out of place here to attempt any such reconstruction at length, and it must suffice if we can indicate briefly some of the main problems, not already discussed, on which it seems possible to arrive at a reasonable conclusion about Plato's views.

1. A few centuries ago many readers of Plato would probably have said that the most important part of his teaching was his theory of Love, and it might plausibly be maintained that this theory has, in fact, had a more powerful influence at certain periods than any other of his teachings at any time. But that does not necessarily mean that Plato himself took it as seriously as did his readers in the sixteenth and seventeenth centuries.

Indeed, it is pretty clear to us now that he did not. Of course, he uses the word ἔρως (*erōs*), which we translate as Love, frequently as a general term for the love of knowledge or goodness which is the driving force behind all our highest endeavour. But the specific point with which we are now concerned, the nature of the love of one individual for another, is only· dealt with in two dialogues, the *Symposium* and the *Phaedrus*, and the form in which the views on the matter are put forward in both dialogues strongly suggests that Plato did not intend to commit himself too seriously to them.

These two dialogues are among the most brilliant expressions of Plato's literary and dramatic genius, and that side of them, particularly in the *Symposium,* is so prominent that there seems something more than usually incongruous in attempting to present a bald summary of the views contained in them. But, in very general terms, the argument seems to be this:—Passionate love for an individual, so far as it is more than a purely physical craving, is to be regarded as a particular expression of certain more general needs or desires. In the first place, there is the yearning for immortality, of which the most obvious expression is the desire to generate children who will carry on something of oneself, and secondly, there is the passion for beauty and the yearning to be in possession of or in contact with it. Both these desires may be aroused in the first place by an individual human being. But it is possible to be led on from that to discover that they can be satisfied much more fully by contact with the realm of eternal realities, the Forms, and by the contemplation of the Absolute Beauty that we can discover there, in just the same way as we can come to see that intellectual curiosity about particular sensible objects must eventually, if it is to be fully satisfied, lead us on to a knowledge of the Forms.

When we ask ourselves how much importance to attach to Plato's views on this question as part of his whole philosophy, besides the general considerations already mentioned, there is a further point to be borne in mind. In both the dialogues the discussion is conducted with special application to the homosexual love between males which was widespread in ancient Greece, and, so far as we can judge, very generally condoned, or at the most mildly reprobated, if not, as was the case in some cities, positively approved. Plato himself always strongly disapproved of physical intercourse between individuals of the same sex. But he recognized the prevalence of the tendency even among men who, in other respects, had the highest potentialities for good. And his discussion of it may be taken as an attempt to show that the desire may, in our modern phraseology, be 'sublimated' into the pursuit of knowledge and goodness. On the other hand, to suppose that this was for him the only, or even the best, way of being led on to this pursuit would be quite contrary to all he says elsewhere, and is not, indeed, seriously suggested in these two dialogues.

About love between man and woman, Plato has not much to say. We may suppose that there, too, the same process of sublimation might take place, as, for instance, between the men and women guardians in the *Republic*. But he generally seems to assume that heterosexual love would normally find its natural expression in physical union, and this he regards as incompatible with the sublimation of it. There is, in Plato, none of the idealization of the sexual act itself which we find in some modern lines of thought. To him it is merely the expression of a normal physical need. There is nothing bad or wrong about it in itself: we find no advocacy of complete celibacy in Plato. But it does require to be controlled and regulated, both for the benefit of society and for the self-discipline and development of the individual. And Plato certainly does advocate a very strict control. The regulations in the *Republic* are repugnant to us today for many reasons. But it is certainly not because they are unduly lax or easy-going. On the contrary, they demand very strict limitations on sexual activity. To speak, as some careless modern writers have done, of 'promiscuity' in this connexion is preposterously wide of the mark. In the *Laws,* strict monogamy is the rule, and Plato expresses strong disapproval of all extra-marital intercourse, though he does not think it practicable to forbid it by law. In general, Plato's views on the question are apt to seem to us somewhat cold-blooded and utilitarian, But in this respect they are not, so far as we can judge, very much out of line with normal Greek ideas on the matter, though they are much stricter on certain points. We need not, however, go so far back for a parallel. For his attitude is in many respects the same as that expressed in the words of our English Prayer Book, so distressingly unromantic to modern taste. The institution of marriage, we read there, is ordained first for the procreation of children, and secondly, as 'a remedy against sin'. Allowing for a somewhat different connotation of the word 'sin', that is very much what Plato means. And, we may add, there are passages in the *Laws* which suggest that he was not unmindful of the 'mutual aid and comfort' which is laid down in the Prayer Book as the third purpose of marriage.

2. Another matter on which there has at times been a good deal of discussion is Plato's theory of art. And the first point to note in that connexion is that Plato has no theory of art, or at least, if he has, it does not appear in his writings. What he does give us in several passages is a discussion of the use of the arts, including literature and music, in education, meaning by that the leading of the mind to true knowledge, and the proper development and harmonization of the emotions. This he regards as the final end of all activity, and any activity that has any effect at all in that direction must be judged by the degree to which it helps or hinders the attainment of this final end. There is no other standard of judgement, independent of this, which can claim validity, at any rate as a guide to action. If we admit that literature or art has any effect on character, and if we admit that the most important thing for anyone is the kind of character he develops, then it seems an inescapable conclusion that, by some means or other, the literature or art produced, particularly that given to young people, should be controlled with this end in mind. Hence the rigid censorship laid down in the *Republic,* and to a milder degree in the *Laws,* on the works of literature which are allowed to be produced.

Plato's attitude has often been sweepingly and unthinkingly condemned by modern writers, and certainly no one nowadays would accept all his detailed provisions. But to understand his general position there are certain considerations to be borne in mind.

In the first place, his argument in these passages only refers to the work of the poets, particularly Homer and Hesiod, based on the traditional myths or legends, which Plato, like many Greeks, regarded as, in the main, fictitious. But fiction, as we all know, without any direct argument or exhortation, can be used to present certain types of conduct or character as admirable and worthy of imitation, and others as the reverse. It is from that point of view that Plato deals with it. Secondly, we must remember that in discussing this type of literature as an agent in moral education, Plato was in line, so far as we can judge, with ordinary Greek ideas. It seems clear that the ancient poets were regarded, in some way and to some degree, as teachers of right conduct, and it was as such that they were made a staple part of ordinary Greek education. Plato is therefore judging them in the light of claims which would commonly be put forward for them. It has sometimes been said that Homer was the Greek Bible. That is very misleading if we are thinking of the orthodox Christian view of the Bible. There was never felt to be any obligation on anyone to accept the Homeric poems as correct statements of fact or even as infallible teachings of moral truths. But Homer and the other older poets were regarded as in some way enshrining the wisdom of the ancients and therefore deserving of a special degree of respect and attention to the lessons that could be learnt from them. This attitude is, in fact, in many ways akin to the attitude towards the Bible of many people at the present day, who have abandoned orthodox Christianity, but retain some degree of respect for the Christian tradition. Or, again, it might be paralleled by the attitude of some more orthodox Christians towards the Old Testament, as distinguished from the New.

One more point remains to be made. If we wanted to make the above parallel closer, we should have to imagine that all our writers of fiction and drama were by custom and tradition confined for their choice of subjects to the stories in the Bible, which they might retell in their own way, but would not be free to alter in their main features. That was the position in which the Greek imaginative writer, particularly the dramatist, in fact, was placed. Except to a very limited degree in comedy, he was confined for his plots to the accepted stock of traditional legends, and could not invent new stories for himself. The idea of fiction as we know it had hardly yet occurred to anyone. This has an important bearing on the question of practical policy. We are as alive as Plato to the fact that certain types of fiction or drama or films can have an unhealthy effect, particularly on young people. But we feel in general that the situation can be met by the production of other work of a healthier tendency, and we rely on a variety of influences to secure that this reaches the quarters where it is needed. This method was hardly open to a Greek of Plato's time, and the only remedy left to him was excision and selection from an existing mass of material.

Another angle from which Plato approached the matter is that of the kind of knowledge of reality that can be gained from art and poetry. What knowledge of reality means to him ought by now to be sufficiently clear. It is only found completely in apprehension of the Forms, but there can be an approximation to it in the knowledge of sensible objects so far as this is assimilated to knowledge of the Forms, particularly by being based on precise measurement and mathematical expression. In a well-known passage in the *Republic*, a sharp contrast is drawn between this kind of knowledge and the sort of information that we can get about an object from a picture of it. The picture, so far from giving the shape or dimensions that exact measurement tells us to belong to the object, deliberately reproduces the illusory aspect seen from a particular angle, and thus turns our minds away even from such knowledge as can be attained of sensible objects. This has sometimes been taken as indicating that Plato took a purely representational view of the function of art. But that is to read much more into the passage than is there. All it says is that so far as a painting is taken as a representation of an object, as giving us information or understanding about it, it is at a very low level of knowledge, akin to the shadows and reflections mentioned in an earlier passage. There is no discussion here, one way or the other, of the possibility that there might be a value in the painting, quite apart from its representation of the original.

The main point of the passage, however, is probably to be looked for in the interesting, but somewhat debatable analogy which Plato draws between this, and the representation in words that we find in literature, which for him in this connexion means poetry. For us the argument would probably be easier to appreciate if we applied it in the first place to prose fiction. The author, he suggests, can imitate in words the external appearance, the characteristic way of talking, for instance, of various sorts of people and their activities, and thus create the illusion that we have been in the presence of, say, a great general, or a man skilled in some other profession. Yet it is pure illusion, for the writer knows nothing in reality of how such a man acquires and exercises his skill, any more than the artist who draws a tool knows how to make, still less to use, the tool itself. If he did he would be a great general himself. We cannot, therefore, learn anything about any of the particular activities of life or about the conduct of life in general from the works of the poets, except certain aspects of its external appearance seen from a particular angle. Any claim made for or by the poets that they can educate us for life is baseless. The most they can do is, as has been seen, to stimulate in us feelings in favour of this or that kind of behaviour. But, as poets, they can stimulate these feelings as easily for the wrong kind of behaviour as for the right, and, if we believe it to be important that the stimulus should be in the right direction, we cannot leave it to the poets to decide, but must have their activities controlled by those with knowledge of the true principles of right conduct.

It would be impossible to discuss all the issues raised in this connexion. We can, for instance, only mention in passing Plato's special objection to the drama as a form of literature. But one general point remains on which something must be said. Is there no other standard, no purely aesthetic standard, by which works of art or literature or music can be judged? There are a number of scattered statements, not always perfectly consistent with each other, which have some bearing on this point. But Plato's general position seems to be that, apart from purely technical dexterity, the only standard of judgement of a work of art as such, irrespective of its effect on character, is the amount of pleasure it gives. That is, indeed, always an essential element in it. At the lowest level there is pure amusement or recreation, pleasure, which has no effect one way or the other on the character. With all his austerity, Plato quite approves of a certain amount of this. It is interesting to note that in the *Laws* he allows occasional performances of knock-about farce, as a sort of comic relief. But most forms of art claim to be more than that. And, if we begin to judge the kind or quality of pleasure that they produce, if we ask, for instance, what element or desire in us they appeal to, then we are back once more at the moral standard. That may be illustrated by one, though not the only one, of Plato's objections to drama. Drama always tends, he maintains, to get its effects by the display of strong emotions. A successful play cannot be made out of quiet self-controlled lives. And the pleasure we get from drama is largely the vicarious satisfaction of displays of un-restrained emotions which we know we ought to, and very likely do, control in our own behaviour. Plato thinks that this pleasure strengthens the emotional tendencies in us and makes them more difficult to control. This was in striking contrast to the well-known view of his pupil, Aristotle, who held that if we could thus relieve ourselves by letting off our emotions in the safe surroundings of the theatre, we worked them out of our system for the time being, and therefore found them much easier to control in ordinary life.

Much the same applies to music, where we should readily recognize that different types of music arouse different moods and appeal to different feelings in us. The application to the visual arts is not so clear. We have already seen that as a means of getting knowledge of reality through imitation, the visual arts took a very low place. But yet we are told, though only very briefly, in the *Republic* that the practitioners of the visual arts must be directed to see that the children, as they grow up, are surrounded by the most beautiful products of these arts that can be made. We may well wonder what standard of beauty Plato had in mind here, and what constituted 'a good picture' from this point of view. It certainly could not lie in the accurate representation of a model. Nor does he tell us anything, as he does in the case of music or literature, of the kinds of emotion or desire to which a piece of painting or sculpture could appeal. He simply speaks in brief general terms of harmony and sym-metry as the prime condition, which he applies, incidentally, to architecture in the same way as to the other visual arts. Per-haps a further clue may be found in a passage in the *Philebus* where he is speaking of the pure pleasures of sight which are included in the most complete good life. Here he tells us that the highest degree of this sort of pleasure is to be found, not in the contemplation of human or animal bodies, but in pure geometrical figures. We must leave it to the artists to work out the possible interpretations of these clues, for Plato gives us no further help. The general impression that he leaves is that, though his own form of imagery was obviously strongly visual, he was not very much interested in the visual arts. And he certainly did not assign to them a place in education in the least comparable to the large and important part played by poetry and music.

3. There is one special point, which is not really important enough for Plato's general position to demand treatment in a work of this length. But as a highly exaggerated importance has been attached to it in some recent criticisms of Plato perhaps a word or two should be said about it. That is his view of the value of truth and his alleged advocacy of the use of falsehood as an instrument of statecraft and education. We may note, in passing, that the word ψεῦδος (pseudos), which is used in this connexion, was applied to any statement that was not literally true, including the fictions of the poets or imaginative writers. The usual translation of it by 'lie', therefore, can often introduce a subtle element of exaggeration into the argument.

Apart from some reference in a small early dialogue of little importance, the *Republic* is the only dialogue in which the subject is discussed at all, and there Plato says that, though truth is of the highest value, there are occasions on which a spoken falsehood or fiction may be necessary 'as a medicine'. He only gives us one or two definite instances of the sort of thing he had in mind. And of these the one that has excited most attention is the myth, which will be familiar to all readers of the *Republic,* of the creation of men out of different metals, which makes them suitable for different kinds of work. He suggests this as a sort of foundation-myth of his city, which should be taught to all citizens, to the rulers as much as to the rest. It is to this myth that Plato applies the phrase usually, though somewhat misleadingly, translated 'noble lie'. The point of the myth is, of course, that it puts the general views about human nature that Plato believes to be true in the form of a concrete story of the creation of man. Such a procedure would not readily occur to us. But then we have not been brought up as the Greeks were, and as the citizens of the *Republic* were to be, on a body of legendary stories, which included stories about our own origins and the origins of other communities. It has at times, however, been suggested in our own day that some of the stories of the Old Testament should be regarded like that, as concrete pictorial presentations of some general moral or religious truths. We may or may not approve of this, but there seems no ground in it for any excessive condemnation of Plato. And, in any case, the importance of this suggestion for the general argument of the *Republic* is not great and has been exaggerated out of all proportion by some modern writers.

But, however we may argue about particular cases, the general principle put forward by Plato would surely not be seriously denied by anyone. Very few, if any, people would be found to assert that there can be no possible occasion on which it would be right to tell a lie. During the Second World War, Mr. Winston Churchill once asserted that it was proper to use language that would deceive the enemy, even if it might mean deceiving one's own people also for the time being. Again there have been times of tension in the past in which governments, anxious to preserve the peace, have exercised a considerable economy of truth in order to avoid rousing popular feeling to a pitch which might make war inevitable, and such action has met with subsequent approval. Occasions such as these are clearly among those referred to in general terms by Plato. And unless one is prepared to assert that such action can never, in any possible circumstances, be legitimate, there are no just grounds for condemning Plato's general principle. We may add, further, that his view appears to be that only those of the highest development of moral character can be trusted to decide when a falsehood is really necessary for the general good. This, like many general principles, is obviously capable of misapplication in practice. But as a general principle it is hard to deny.

4. A good deal has already been said about Plato's views on education. Indeed, a great part of his writings might be des-

cribed, in one sense, as a treatise on education. For the primary interest that he has in mind throughout is the question of how to produce the right kind of character and the right attitude of mind. But it may none the less be useful here to bring together some of his general ideas on education, in the strict sense, which have not yet been explicitly touched on.

It has sometimes been said that Plato's system of education was devised to meet the requirements of a leisured class. There is a certain amount of truth in this as applied to the account in the *Laws,* though even there it is by no means the whole truth. But as applied to the *Republic* the statement is quite untrue. The scheme of education there is directed towards the training, not of a leisured class, but of a busy class of rulers and civil and military administrators. In that sense, his system of education is practical and vocational, and its object is to train people to do their work in the community efficiently. But, at any rate as regards the training for these higher functions, this practical result will not be attained unless, in the course of their training, the students come to value the knowledge of the subjects studied for its own sake. That is one general idea of Plato's which is well worth thinking over, in its application to higher studies in our own day.

The general idea of vocational education, in the broad sense of suiting the training to the particular aptitudes and levels of ability of the pupils, is central in Plato's thought on the subject. We are not told anything directly in the *Republic* of the education of the other classes besides the guardians. Obviously the technical instruction in the crafts for which they showed aptitude would begin early, but there are some reasons for thinking it possible that the early stages of the basic education would be common to all classes. Or else there might be differences within the same class in this respect, according to the craft or trade for which the children were destined.

There is a point that is worth making in this connexion, even at the risk of a certain degree of irrelevance. It is commonly said that Plato despised all the crafts or technical skills, and there are certainly passages in which he speaks slightingly of them, particularly as a preparation for political activity. This attitude, incidentally, was widespread in ancient Greece, and is noted

as practically universal by Herodotus a generation or so before Plato's time. But Plato himself was not always perfectly
consistent in this, and there are other passages which suggest
a different attitude. He certainly had a considerable interest
in and knowledge of the details of technical processes, if we can
judge by the number of times he uses them as illustrations of
his argument. There is an interesting passage in the *Philebus*
in which he grades the different crafts in accordance with their
approximation to true scientific knowledge. Among the highest
he puts the arts, such as those of the builder or the carpenter,
which use precise measurement and calculation, and he ranks
them, for that reason, higher even than the art of the general.
Of the higher technical skills, such as that of the doctor or the
navigator, he never speaks with anything but respect, though
they do not, of course, rise to the true knowledge of the philosopher. We must not, then, think of Plato as indiscriminately
dismissing all crafts and skills as equally unworthy of notice,
and it is reasonable to suppose that the education for some of
them would have a good deal in common with the early stages
of the education for the philosopher-ruler.

To revert to our main argument, it is in connexion with this
general doctrine that we must consider the bearing of a well-
known passage in the *Republic*. That is the passage in Book VII,
where he says that education does not consist in putting knowledge into the soul, 'as if one were to put sight into blind eyes',
but in turning the soul which has the capacity for knowledge
in the right direction. This is often quoted as meaning that
Plato disapproved of the mere giving of information and
thought that the pupils must be brought to see things for
themselves. This undoubtedly represents Plato's point of view
correctly, but it is not the point that he is primarily concerned
with in this passage. The point here is that the intelligence, or
the capacity for knowing and understanding, is something
given to us, in fixed quantity, by nature, and cannot itself be
increased or strengthened by training, as we can strengthen a
muscle by exercise. All we can do by training is to turn these
powers in the right direction, just as we cannot normally
strengthen our eyesight by more use of it, but can be trained
to look for this or that object, or in this or that direction. The

corollary of that is, of course, that if we have not got the natural ability to grasp the highest or most difficult truths, we cannot be taught to do so, and had better learn to turn the abilities that we have in a direction appropriate to them.

But the essential point is the direction of interest. And the direction of interest is not something that can be dealt with in isolation, but is a function of the whole personality and character and, in particular, of the general point of view about what sorts of thing are or are not worth while. That is what the earlier stages of education, in music and literature, seek to instil, not by direct precept so much as by the general atmosphere implied in the poems and songs that are studied. That is the basis on which the educator at the higher stages has to work. His task is to discover the native ability and interest, to remove unfavourable influences, and to lead it in the direction in which it can most fully satisfy itself.

In the light of this we can well understand Plato's frequently expressed dislike of compulsion in the serious part of education. He did not, of course, believe, like some modern educationists, in leaving the young with no guidance or control at all. But the control is much more negative, in keeping certain things away from them, than positive, in telling them to do this or that. Thus we are told both in the *Republic* and the *Laws* that mathematics, the foundation of serious advanced studies, must be introduced to the children in the first place by means of games and puzzles involving mathematical calculation, so that they begin by thinking of it as a pleasing amusement, not a wearisome task. And that is part of a wider consideration, namely the great importance that Plato attaches, particularly in his latest writings, to play and games. Indeed, the whole of the education in 'music and gymnastic' tends more and more to take the form of organized games. And here we have what might seem a paradox were it not so thoroughly familiar among ourselves. For Plato play is certainly not spontaneous uncontrolled individual expression. Its form is controlled by the law as rigidly as the M.C.C. controls the rules of cricket. And it seems, indeed, as if Plato, like us, looked largely to organized games, and also, of course, to the strictly military part of training, for the element of order and discipline in education. The higher intellectual training is much more a matter for free individual activity. At any rate, Plato makes it clear, in a passage to which we shall recur later, that true philosophical knowledge cannot be simply transmitted by one person to another, still less, of course, imposed by one person on another. It can only be grasped by each person for himself after unstinted argument and counter-argument and question and answer.

5. There are several questions, on which a good deal more might be said, that arise in connexion with Plato's views on the nature of knowledge and the processes of thought. We have already had occasion to say something about these views so far as they were connected with the Theory of Forms. But here particularly there is a good deal that can be discussed up to a point independently of this theory, because this is one of the general questions noted at the beginning of this chapter in which Plato was so largely concerned with the discussion of current views and current controversies. It is interesting to note how often in the course of these discussions issues are raised and views put forward which are startlingly like some of those familiar to us at the present day or in the immediate past. But, interesting though these points of resemblance are, it would be a mistake to exaggerate them. There is no doubt that some commentators in recent years have gone seriously astray by attempting to restate Plato's argument completely in terms of contemporary doctrine.[1] Similarly, some of his critics have equally gone astray by blaming him for not having anticipated all the problems and difficulties that have arisen in contemporary discussions.

To discuss all these points properly would need a prolonged treatment and could, indeed, be given a volume in itself. We can hardly do more here than attempt to list some of the most interesting topics discussed. That fascinating dialogue, the *Theaetetus*, is entirely devoted to a critical discussion of some current theories of knowledge, and, while revealing their weaknesses, arrives at no positive conclusion itself. It begins by discussing and dismissing the claims of sense-perception

[1] Some well-founded criticisms of attempts of this kind may be found in F. M. Cornford's *Plato's Theory of Knowledge*.

to be knowledge. In the course of this discussion there is an examination of Protagoras' doctrine of the relativity of knowledge to the individual, a doctrine which has many points of resemblance to at least some formulations of the modern theory known as Pragmatism. In the days when Pragmatism was still a burning question the *Theaetetus* was a veritable quarry of ammunition for both sides in the controversy. It then goes on to a discussion of the idea that knowledge is true opinion or belief, and gets entangled, for the greater part of this section, in the discussion of the nature of untrue opinion or error. If true belief is correctly described as thinking what is, it would seem that false belief must consist in thinking what is not. But 'what is not' is nothing. Yet how can we think nothing? Thinking nothing is simply not thinking. This difficulty, again, has reappeared in modern philosophical writing, as have also some of the suggested solutions of it put forward, and rejected, in the *Theaetetus*.

This same problem, along with several others, reappears in the *Sophist*, and here we also get a discussion of the negative judgement, about which certain difficulties had been raised in Greek speculation. Plato's account of this, very briefly, is that the words 'is not' in a negative judgement do not imply a mere negation, a denial of being, but assert a positive relation, a relation of exclusion or 'otherness' between two terms which stand for something real. Similarly the false judgement is not merely 'thinking what is not', but is asserting a relation between two terms other than the relation which in fact subsists between them. A point of great interest, which is dealt with all too briefly by Plato here, is his general account of the nature of the judgement or unit of thought, which he here indicates by the word δόξα (*doxa*). This is an entirely different use of the term from that with which we are familiar in connexion with the Theory of Forms, where it stands for 'opinion' or 'belief' as distinguished from knowledge. This is an interesting indication that Plato's logical theory was being developed to some degree independently of the Theory of Forms. To summarize still further an already summary account, we may say that his general view is that the judgement is not something that can be considered in isolation, but is essentially the conclusion of a process. More specifically, the typical form of the process is that of question and answer, and a judgement is always an answer to a question. It is tempting to link up what Plato says here with certain contemporary discussions, for instance, the distinction made by a modern writer between 'the logic of propositions' and 'the logic of question-and-answer'. So far as Plato could understand the distinction, he would clearly have inclined towards the view suggested in the latter phrase. But it would be out of place to attempt any further development of this line of thought here.

One more point of importance deserves a brief mention. That is the account, to which some reference has already been made, of the nature of philosophical thinking in the Seventh Letter. Again, we must summarize very briefly a long, and in places obscure, argument. But the general conclusion that emerges is that the results of philosophical thinking cannot be set out in a series of general propositions, which can be conveyed from one person to another without regard to the processes by which they have been reached. On the contrary, they can only be grasped by each man for himself, after going at length through much the same processes. Before he can begin to understand philosophical conclusions, he must go through a prolonged examination of his experience, the use of language, the evidence of sense-perception, and so on, by the method in the phrase already quoted, of 'friendly argument and counter-argument and unstinted question and answer'. And at the end the conclusions 'shine out' or, as we should say, 'dawn on us', and light up the whole of our experience. If I have not misunderstood Plato, this seems to me a profoundly true account of the nature of philosophical thought.[1]

The particular occasion for this discussion is Plato's wish to explain that he has never set out his philosophical conclusions in written form, nor authorized anyone else to do so. Though we may feel that he exaggerates the impossibility of

[1] For the development of a view of the nature of philosophy, which I believe to be fundamentally akin to that expressed here by Plato, I may perhaps be permitted to refer to an article of my own on 'The Examination of Assumptions' which appeared in the *Proceedings of the Aristotelian Society* for 1934–5 and was reprinted in my *Studies in Philosophy*.

this, it is not difficult to see the considerations that might have led him to this point of view. For us the special interest of this passage is that it makes much clearer to us what it is that we are reading when we read Plato's dialogues. It was suggested in our first chapter that Plato himself took his dialogues much less seriously than we are inclined to do. And that is perfectly true if we treat them as an exposition of his philosophical conclusions. But if we treat them as an attempt to stimulate a certain state of mind, to direct our thoughts to certain aspects of our experience and to open up possible lines of speculation, in a word to put us on the road along which we might eventually come to arrive at these conclusions for ourselves, then the case is altered. There is no doubt that he did attach considerable value to them for this purpose, and in the *Laws* he recommends his own, and similar, dialogues as useful reading for certain stages of higher education.

There are many other points on which it would be tempting to linger. There are several indications in the dialogues of Plato's keen interest in the nature and structure of language. In the *Sophist* we have the beginnings not only of the logical, but also of the grammatical, analysis of the sentence. The difference between noun and verb is clearly laid down, and, though the terms used for these parts of speech occur earlier, it is possible that the explicit distinction between their respective functions is something new. There is also some evidence that the first notions of what we should now think of as a dictionary of the language were conceived in the Academy under Plato's inspiration. So the Platonic Academy may have been, in this respect, the prototype of the French Academy. In an interesting, but somewhat neglected dialogue, the *Cratylus,* Plato discusses two current theories of the nature of language, more particularly of the process of naming. One theory held that names belonged to things 'by nature', the other that they were the product of purely arbitrary convention. Plato discusses both these views and raises what he seems to regard as fatal objections to them as they stand. No positive alternative view is put forward, but the conclusion that the argument seems to point to is that, while there is clearly a large element of arbitrary convention in actual languages, we must not lose sight of the possibility that some languages or systems of nomenclature might be better adapted for expressing the real nature of things than others. There might therefore be a real standard, if not exactly of right and wrong, at least of good and bad for languages. But the point is not developed, and a great part of the dialogue is devoted to etymological speculations, some of which are clearly not meant to be taken very seriously.

It would be tempting, also, to say a good deal more about Plato's relation to natural science, if only because of the profound misunderstandings which mark much modern writing on the subject. Something has already been said on this matter in a previous chapter. Here we can only add one or two points. It is not in the least true that Plato, in any sense or degree, disapproved of investigation in natural science, though undoubtedly he thought that other studies were of higher value. He disapproved of the materialist metaphysics adopted by some scientists. But that is a very different matter. Again, it is entirely untrue that Plato thought that the facts of nature could be deduced *a priori* from some abstract universal principles, without the need for observation. That is not only untrue, it is the exact opposite of what he says. If it were true, it would break down the distinction between the sensible and intelligible worlds so fundamental to his doctrine.

What is true is that Plato was not himself much concerned with detailed scientific research. When knowledge of the facts of nature was needed for his argument, as in the *Timaeus,* he generally relied on those whom he regarded as recognized authorities, Empedocles, the medical writers collected under the name of Hippocrates, and so on. He was, of course, deeply concerned with the general nature and presuppositions of scientific knowledge. And the conclusions on this point which emerged from his general philosophical position formed a very good basis for much scientific development. We have already referred to the importance attached to precise measurement and expression in mathematical terms. Besides that, there is the stress laid, particularly in the later dialogues, on the importance of correct principles of definition, division, and classification, which provided a stimulus for the beginnings of scientific classification of the species of plants and animals. We are most familiar with this in the work of Aristotle, but he was by no means alone among Plato's pupils in following this interest. Indeed, there is some evidence that investigation of this kind had already been initiated in the Academy under Plato.

In the development of mathematics, Plato's services are incontestable. Later tradition attributed to him personally certain discoveries in mathematical method. It is certain that the great developments in Greek mathematics which marked the half-century or so which followed the foundation of the Academy were almost entirely the work of that school. In the associated science of astronomy, also, much original work was done in Plato's school. He himself held certain astronomical views, the details of which are obscure. There has been much dispute, for instance, as to whether he thought the earth moved, and, if he did, what sort of motion he ascribed to it, or as to whether he thought that the earth was the centre of the universe, and, if he did not, what body he put in that place. But these are details into which it is impossible to enter here.

There are other points of interest on which something might be said. But this is, perhaps, enough to show the wide field of subjects over which Plato's mind ranged, and the varied contributions that his thought made to them, either directly through his own ideas, or through the stimulus that he gave to his followers.

10
Plato Today

SO FAR we have been occupied with the attempt to understand what Plato meant. No attempt has been made, except occasionally and incidentally, to evaluate his views as a possible contribution to our own thinking. It is true, of course, that our approach throughout has been based on an attempt to see things from Plato's point of view, and to present the argument as it might have presented itself to him if he had been writing in our own time. But that simply means that we have been trying to understand him. Unless we are ready to start with that approach to a philosopher, we cannot begin to understand him at all, and any criticism that we attempt of him will be futile. On the other hand, that certainly does not mean that we have to agree with everything he says. When we have gone as far as we can along this road to understanding, then, and not till then, we can properly begin to ask ourselves what value we can find in his ideas for our own thought.

I have purposely put the question in that form rather than in the more familiar form of asking whether we think his views right or wrong, because it seems to me to express a much more fruitful line of approach. There is a popular assumption that to get anything of value out of a philosopher we must be able to extract from his works a series of definite propositions which we can accept as true in preference to another set of propositions that we had previously accepted and are now prepared to abandon. But, in fact, the formation of genuine philosophical opinion rarely, if ever, proceeds like that at all. We shall never get very far in it if we persist in adopting the attitude of a schoolmaster marking off his pupil's sums as right or wrong. The more we try to understand any serious thinker the less shall we feel inclined to dismiss his ideas as simply false, or, for the matter of that, to accept them just as they stand as absolutely true. We value him for the degree to which he illuminates our own experience and shows us the significance of aspects of it which we had not properly realized. He may stimulate us to become conscious of and re-examine critically things that we have been taking for granted. He may reveal logical conclusions and hidden implications in arguments which we had been accustomed to follow without realizing all they involved, and connexions or contradictions between ideas which we had previously entertained without any realization of the relations between them. In all these and many other ways he may open up for us lines of thought which we can pursue for ourselves in our own way. Of course, our own lines of thought can run parallel with his for a greater or lesser distance or diverge to a greater or lesser extent. In that sense, we may be said relatively to 'agree' or 'disagree' with him. But the value we can get from him is largely independent of that.

Of no philosopher is this truer than of Plato. And that needs particularly to be borne in mind by us, who, in the main, only know him through his dialogues. We have already seen what the purpose of these dialogues is, and how they differ from other philosophical writing. We may say broadly that most philosophers aim at presenting their conclusions to us in systematic form, and we often find it difficult to discover the processes of thought that they went through to arrive at them. Plato, on the other hand, presents us in his dialogues with, as it were, sections, greater or smaller, of the processes that his mind was going through, and our difficulty is much more often to discover the conclusions that they eventually led him to. And that, it may be suggested, is one of the great merits of Plato's writings as an instrument for the teaching of philosophy.

The situation is not so very different when we turn to what we know, or can reasonably conjecture, about Plato's influence on those with whom he was directly in contact. What is certain is that the Academy was never anything in the nature of a church with an established body of doctrine which was to be accepted and handed down to subsequent generations. Of course, Plato had definite opinions of his own, and he clearly hoped that others who would take the trouble to traverse the same ground would eventually arrive at very similar conclusions for themselves. It is, however, doubtful how far this in fact happened. Naturally any body of people working closely and continuously together over a long period would develop a good deal in common in their opinions and points of view. But we have evidence of lively differences of opinion in the Academy even during Plato's lifetime, and certainly after his death each of his associates went his own way. The Academy itself in the course of the next few generations seems to have changed, not only the opinions held by its leading members, but even the kind of question that they were interested in discussing. It is evident that there was never any kind of *depositum fidei* to which the advocates of different views could make appeal. It is not till centuries later, when the tradition of true philosophical inquiry had almost died out, that we find doctrines supported not so much because the arguments for them were sound as because they were supposed to represent what Plato really meant. And, as one might expect, by that stage the capacity to understand what Plato really meant had been very largely lost.

It is very much the same when we consider Plato's general influence on thought in all ages. From one point of view there has often been a tendency to exaggerate this. Indeed, truly fantastic claims have been made, both by admirers and detractors, for the extent of his influence, and he has been held responsible for many things for which in fact he had little or no responsibility at all. In fact, it would be very hard to pick out any definite set of ideas or any particular feature of European thought and say that this was primarily and directly due to the influence of Plato. On the other hand, from a different point of view few, if any, philosophers have had so much influence as Plato, in the effect they produce by challenge and stimulus and suggestion on the individual students of their work. Hardly anyone who reads Plato, particularly with any serious effort at understanding him, thinks in quite the same way after he has read him as he did before. But the change is not necessarily in the direction of Plato's own ideas. Sometimes it may be, quite consciously, a development in opposition to Plato. Sometimes it may be a development, suggested by a study of Plato, but recognized as going much beyond anything Plato ever actually thought. And often in the past a similar process has taken place without being recognized, and thinkers have claimed the authority of Plato for the most diverse views. Indeed, we must recognize that in all the wealth of philosophical ideas and suggestions that there is in Plato, it is possible to find something to support a wide variety of different schools of thought. Yet it would not be much of a paradox to say that Plato has often exercised his greatest influence on those who have misunderstood him. And that, we may add, applies as often to those who thought they were criticizing him as to those who thought they were following him.

In our own day, particularly in this country, the study of Plato has been widespread and intense over a long period of years. And his influence, whether by way of attraction or repulsion, has been correspondingly great. On the one side, there has been a long series of careful scholarly investigations which have put us in a better position for understanding what Plato really meant than any preceding age. On the other, there has been an intensified sense, particularly in recent years, of the bearing of some aspects of Plato's thought on our own problems. Discussions of it from this point of view have sometimes been enlightening. But, as we shall see directly, to look at it too exclusively from this angle may have its dangers, and give rise to a good deal of misunderstanding and misrepresentation.

When we consider the different aspects of Plato's thought we find, as we might expect, a considerable difference between them in the extent to which they have been regarded as relevant to our modern problems. The metaphysical doctrine, the Theory of Forms, in its first phase would probably, as it stands, not make much appeal to modern thought, though interesting parallels to it have occurred here and there. But a serious effort to understand it is well worth while, because it shows that the questions that Plato was trying to answer are recurrent problems that have to be dealt with in our own time as much as in his. Thus the difficulties that he found in accepting sense-perception as a form of knowledge are real difficulties that have to be faced by any serious thinker. In our own day attempts have been made to solve them by an elaborate analysis into sensa, sense-data, sensible objects, and the like. Whether or not these attempts provide a satisfactory solution, they certainly take us as far away from the simple view of common sense as Plato does. Then, again, the aspect of the theory which probably would have seemed the most important to Plato himself, the attempt to find a metaphysical basis in reality for the objective validity of moral judgements, is a problem which has to be faced by any serious thinker. But the modern attempts to solve this problem have in general gone on different lines from Plato's. Some, for instance, have sought to find the basis in the Absolute of Bradley and Bosanquet, others in the belief in a perfect God, from whose being, in some way, both Nature and the moral law take their rise. Neither of these doctrines is Platonic, though it is possible to trace affinities with Plato in both of them.

When we come to the later developments of Plato's metaphysical thought, the situation is more complicated. Certain aspects of this at certain periods have been regarded with great respect, more respect, in fact, than understanding. Thus in the earlier Middle Ages the *Timaeus,* which was much better known than any of the other dialogues, was thought of as an adumbration of revealed truth, because it taught the doctrine of the creation of the world by God. In fact, as we have already seen, the 'creation' in the *Timaeus* is something very different from the creation of Christian doctrine, at any rate in its medieval form. Again, the argument for the existence of God from the fact of motion found its way into the classical proofs, which the Scholastics developed and Kant refuted. But further inspection shows that it was not really quite the same argument, and it was a very different sort of God whose existence was in question. In any case, this particular argument is one of those which make least appeal to modern thought. With regard to Plato's general religious doctrine, it is hard to say what sort of appeal this might make to people of the present day if they could, as it were, look at it afresh on its merits. But that is rarely, if ever, possible. For, with our centuries of Christian tradition, religious doctrine means, for nearly all of us, either some form of Christianity or nothing. And Plato's doctrine cannot be brought into harmony with any form of Christianity. Yet there may be elements in it that might correspond to some sides of our religious experience. Pope's hackneyed lines,

> All are but parts of one stupendous whole,
> Whose body Nature is and God the soul,

doubtless express a view that makes and has made its appeal to many, and, so far as any summary can, these lines express in a vague and general way a view very similar to Plato's.

The other aspects of Plato's final metaphysic are, as we have seen, obscure and difficult. And their influence has never extended beyond very narrow limits, because few people, except professional Platonic scholars, have been ready to take the trouble to understand them. But those who have, have found a rich store of ideas which they could work up in developing their own philosophy. Two of the most distinguished constructive metaphysicians of our time in this country have expressed their indebtedness to Plato. Samuel Alexander, in certain aspects of his system, was avowedly following lines of thought suggested to him by Plato, though the final result was on many points different. And A. N. Whitehead attributed some of the most important features of his own philosophy to an expansion of ideas contained in the *Timaeus*. It is interesting to note that these thinkers, one partly and the other mainly, approached their philosophy in the first place from the study of mathematics, and both were greatly influenced by modern developments in physics. And there is some reason to think that anyone who approached philosophy from the point of view of physical science would, if he took the trouble to understand Plato's theories, find in them much which would provide a congenial background for the development of scientific thought.

But the chief point of impact of Plato's ideas on modern thought has been, as one might expect, his political and social theory. And that has come to us, in the main, through the *Republic*, with an occasional side-glance at the *Laws*. The stimulating and fruitful ideas in the *Politicus*, for instance, have been almost entirely neglected. But the *Republic* during the last half-century or so has probably been studied in this country more widely and more continuously than any single philosophical work by any author. And the varying reactions to it at different times throughout this period provide an interesting chapter in the history of thought.

In the days before the First World War the predominant climate of thought here, and to a greater or lesser degree in most civilized countries, might be broadly described as evolutionary. We tended to believe in something that we called 'progress', conceived of as a continuous process of development by a series of small steps brought about by the contributions of countless people each dealing with the particular problem that faced him at the time. We had, in general, some sort of faith that this process would naturally tend to work out for the good of humanity, though what form that 'good' would take we did not feel called upon to picture to ourselves, except in the most general terms, nor did we think of it as something subject to choice or control by individuals. The task of the statesman was, primarily, by constant attention to secure the conditions under which this process could go on, and that was a matter, before all, of dealing with immediate problems as they arose and removing obvious evils as opportunity offered itself. Of course, this left room for all sorts of fierce differences of opinion on practical policies. But these developed within the framework of this general view, which would have been, consciously or unconsciously, widely adopted by people of the most diverse political connexions.

To those of us who were brought up in that atmosphere the study of the *Republic* came, in the first place, as a challenge and a stimulus to the conscious use of reason in the control and guidance of political and social development. Those who felt that our chief need was, in the words of H. G. Wells, to 'remedy the lack of constructive design in the world' found inspiration in the *Republic*. Wells, himself, was at one period of his thought greatly influenced by Plato, and his book, *A Modern Utopia*, was avowedly an attempt to develop some of the main ideas of the *Republic* into a form in which they could be applied to a modern world-state. The book is still worth reading, if only as an illustration of the way in which Platonic ideas can work in the mind of a modern thinker.

There were other general ideas in Plato that had their influence on us then. But the more concrete and detailed arguments were apt to seem to us a little remote, because they were developed against a background both of ideas and of political and social conditions which was so different from our own at that time. In that respect more recent years have seen a great change, and the world has become much more like the Greek world of Plato's day than any previous period. Many of the political phenomena which Plato had in mind are now as familiar to us as they were to him, whereas forty years ago they would have seemed to us vague and theoretical possibilities of little practical interest. The overthrow of democracies, the rise of 'tyrannies' or dictatorships, the establishment of 'planned societies' as ruthless and totalitarian as that of Sparta —these and similar things we have learnt to know, no longer as 'old, unhappy far-off things' which could not happen now, but as imminent possibilities or as active aspirations or as established realities. The result is that Plato now, as never before, seems often to be talking about much the same kind of situation as we are, and his ideas come to us with a vividness and actuality which they could never have had forty or fifty years ago.

This has obviously brought many advantages for the study of Plato. But it has also brought certain disadvantages, at any rate from the point of view of those who are seriously interested in trying to understand correctly the thought of a past age. For there has been a tendency, in some quarters, to push the parallels much too far, and to treat Plato simply as a participant, on one side or the other, in the controversies of the present day. And some writers, who have found it difficult to fit him in on their own side in these controversies, have identified him completely with the side of their opponents, with the result that he has been treated, not as a serious thinker to be understood, but as an enemy to be attacked, with all the vigour of invective and insinuation that we associate with the bitterest party warfare. One might well go further and say that a good many of the attacks on Plato which have appeared in recent years have been carried on with a degree of misrepresentation, mis-statement and misquotation which ought to discredit even a party politician. It would be easy to give a detailed catalogue of these things, but that would be out of place here. Suffice it to say that anyone who reads these works would be well advised to compare their statements on any specific point very carefully with the original evidence before accepting them as correct. It is a pity that in contemporary controversies on the subject so much time has to be spent in correcting gross and obvious misrepresentations of Plato that it becomes difficult to attempt a serious evaluation of his thought.

The genuine exponent of Plato is, it must be admitted, in something of a dilemma here. On the one hand, it is highly desirable not to weaken the interest and sense of relevance of Plato's thought to our own which this close parallelism to contemporary discussions gives. On the other, one of the advantages of the study of political ideas in a past age is that it ought to make it easier for us to consider dispassionately the value of the ideas as ideas, and we lose that advantage if we introduce all the passions and emotions of our present controversies into their study. For the teacher, perhaps, the best policy is to start by emphasizing, possibly even over-emphasizing, the parallels and by expounding Plato's argument as far as possible in terms of contemporary ideas. But he would soon begin to insinuate the notion that Plato was a real person with a background and problems of his own, which were just as important for him as ours are for us. And his hearers might then gradually become sufficiently interested in this person to feel that it was worth while for its own sake to try to find out about him and his sur-roundings, so that they could look at his problems through his own eyes and see his theories as they presented themselves to him. The more clearly we can picture to ourselves the situa-tion in which Plato wrote and the nearer we can come to putting ourselves at his point of view, the more we shall see that, though his ideas have often points of resemblance to those familiar to us today, they are never quite the same, and to treat them as such is to misrepresent them. But that does not mean that the study of them is of any the less value for us. On the contrary, to analyse the differences is often more illuminating for our own thinking than to concentrate on the resemblances. We must do justice to both sides if we are to get the best out of the study of Plato.

There are various pitfalls that we have to avoid if we are to do this successfully. One, which is often not avoided, is the danger of exaggerating the importance of a particular statement, just because it happens to chime in with our own experience, either our individual experience or that of our own time and society. Yet the statement may be merely a casual remark thrown out in passing and in no way essential to the rest of the argument. There is no reason, of course, why we should not notice these things with interest. But it is a great mistake to see them out of all proportion with the rest. It is certainly a mistake which is often committed, both by admirers of Plato, who wish to claim his support for some line of thought of their own, and by his modern denigrators, who are anxious to emphasize anything that they can find to his discredit. It is particularly important to remember this in reading the *Republic*. For there, undoubtedly, in order to give a concrete and living picture, Plato often puts in details in his proposals which are not in the least an essential part of the general argument. But, in reading any of the dialogues, it has to be remembered that they all, to a greater or lesser degree, take the form of conversations, and it is primarily as conversations that they must be judged, not as the complete and final presentation of a systematic philosophy, still less as the official programme of a political party. But this point, perhaps, has already been sufficiently emphasized.

A kindred point, on which it is important but difficult to keep a due balance, is in the matter of judging Plato against the background of his own time. Of course, in a general way it is obvious that to understand him at all we have to think of him as a Greek writing in fourth-century Athens and not as an Englishman writing at the present day. But the application of this in detail is open to many subtle possibilities of error. Plato, like every other thinker, was largely a child of his age. And we often find him, in the course of his writings, apparently taking for granted certain ideas or other features of the civilization of his time which are different from ours. Some of these may attract us, others may repel us. But we certainly must not allot either praise or blame to them in just the same proportions as we should if they were put forward now by a writer of the present day. In any case, we should probably not for long remain content with the over-simplified attitude of facile praise and blame, and should begin to look for the ideas in Plato which seem to be most fruitful in suggesting possibilities for our own thought. And in that search it is essential to distinguish between ideas which were consciously adopted as an essential part of his argument, and those which were assumed, more or less unconsciously, because they were part of the climate of thought at the time. These latter do not always and necessarily cohere with the rest of the argument, and may, indeed, on occasions be a positive obstruction to it.

In some modern writers, the attempt to apply Plato's political ideas to the present age has taken the form of a comparison between the constitution of the *Republic* and that of various actual states that exist or have existed. At a relatively elementary stage that, if fairly done, may be a useful exercise in analysis, though it runs the risk of concentrating attention too much on the detailed provisions to the neglect of the general ideas behind them. But it is a difficult thing to do fairly, and when, as in some writers, it takes the form of trying to imagine what Plato would have said about this or that modern constitution, it can never be more than a series of highly hazardous guesses. For the scheme in the *Republic* was an ideal, which Plato did not expect to see ever fully realized, and which he certainly would not have regarded as being realized in any modern state. Which of the various fallings away from it in modern states he would have regarded least unfavourably, and what steps he would have thought would be likely to produce the nearest approximation to it in our very different conditions, are questions on which those who have studied Plato most deeply would be the least likely to pronounce with any confidence.

Some of the guesses that have been made certainly seem pretty wide of the mark. To suggest, as has occasionally been done, that Plato would have approved of the Fascist or Nazi régimes is really preposterous. In fact, these régimes provided an almost complete analogue to the Greek 'tyranny', which Plato always regarded as the lowest and most degraded form of state, and there are remarkably close parallels between the careers of Hitler and Mussolini and the account of the rise of the typical tyrant in the *Republic*. Nor would it be easy to think of any body of people more unlike the guardians of the *Republic* than the Fascist or Nazi leaders. Plato might very likely have found much more to approve of in the rule of the Communist Party in Russia, and it would be possible to point out a number of significant resemblances between the Soviet Republic and the Republic of Plato. It would be equally possible to think of points of which Plato would probably have disapproved. We must remember, in this connexion, that it is a profound fallacy to suppose that, because Plato gave his ideal philosopher-rulers absolute authority, he would therefore have approved of any constitution which gave absolute authority to any select body of rulers. On the contrary, it was only because they were ideal rulers that the guardians were fit to be entrusted with absolute powers, and the further any other body of rulers fell away from these ideal qualifications the more would their powers need to be restricted. It is therefore quite possible that Plato would have looked with greater favour on some of the more successful parliamentary democracies of our own time, where the element of democracy, allowed for in the *Laws,* is tempered by the existence of a recognized body of political leaders and by a professional civil service. As we go further back in history other parallels suggest themselves, particularly the cases in which a greater or lesser degree of authority has been in the hands of a religious body. For there are obvious points of resemblance between the guardians and a religious order. But it would be unprofitable here to pursue these uncertain speculations further.

Of much more profit is it to consider some of the general ideas at the back of the detailed provisions, and to ask ourselves what sort of stimulus or challenge they can provide for our own thought. That, of course, is a task that, in the final resort, everyone must undertake for himself. The primary purpose of this work is to give some help by showing what Plato's main ideas were, leaving it to the reader to find out for himself whether these ideas contribute anything to the development of his own thinking. But it may not be out of place, before concluding, to make one or two suggestions about the ways in which Plato's ideas may act as a stimulus to our own.

Take, for instance, Plato's criticism of democracy, which has aroused such obloquy in some recent writings. What is the fundamental idea at the back of that? As we have seen, to put it very summarily, it is his picture of the ideal society in which everyone pursues the vocation for which his natural qualities most fit him, and devotes his whole energies to it for the benefit of the whole. That is recognized as the condition of efficiency in nearly all pursuits. And Plato asks why the same should not apply to the work of ruling, the most important and the most difficult of all, which should demand the highest natural abilities and the most careful and thorough training.

This is an argument that deserves the most serious consideration, and it cannot be dismissed by calling Plato names, or by imputing motives to him. For whatever his motives, the ideas remain, and in our own day we have in practice gone a good way to meet them. Indeed, a modern representative democracy might fairly be described as a compromise between, or a synthesis of, Greek democratic ideas and Plato's criticisms of them. In any case, to consider Plato's arguments fairly would force us to analyse and clarify our own views. We should have, for instance, to make clear to ourselves whether we consider government by perfect rulers, as envisaged by Plato, to be an ideal which is, unfortunately, incapable of realization because of the impossibility of finding rulers who would really fulfil the qualifications necessary, so that in practice it would be safer to rely on some admixture of democracy. With such a line of argument Plato would very likely have felt a good deal of sympathy. On the other hand, we might well feel that, even as an ideal, there is something in democracy which Plato missed, so that even in a perfect state there would have to be a considerable element of it. In that case, it would be an invaluable exercise to have to ask ourselves exactly what that 'something' is. And when we had answered that question, we should have to go on to develop our notions of what the proper relations between the democratic element and its leaders and experts

are. Again, on the question of moral leadership and the responsibility for setting the moral standards of the community, a
study of Plato should do much to stir up our own thinking. At
the least it might save us from the hypocrisy of pretending that
there is no such thing. But whether it should be acknowledged
or unacknowledged, what the proper qualifications for it are,
what its relation is to political leadership and authority—all
these, and others like them, are problems which are worthy
of careful consideration. And we can hardly study Plato at all
deeply without beginning to consider them.

One could go on indefinitely with the list of ideas which a
study of Plato should bring to our attention. But, perhaps, as
a last point a word might be said about his alleged totalitarianism. Of course the word 'totalitarian' nowadays is in danger
of becoming merely a substitute for thought, and, in any case,
any attempt to classify a thinker of the standing of Plato under
some abstract '-ism' should be regarded with the deepest
suspicion. But one knows quite well what those who accuse him
of totalitarianism have in mind, though they often greatly exaggerate it. It is to be remembered that in the *Republic* the provisions for censorship and restriction are only mentioned in
connexion with imaginative literature, poetry and fiction,
and also with music. Indeed, it is probably the creative artist
who would have most grounds for complaint against Plato,
though experience of past ages seems to suggest that fairly rigid
restrictions by custom and convention on the permitted art-
forms may sometimes be compatible with a high level of artistic
achievement. Nothing is said about any restriction on the free
discussion of ideas or research into facts. It is only at the end
of his life, when writing the *Laws,* that Plato came to advocate
a very limited degree of suppression of opinion, a much
smaller degree, incidentally, than the law laid down in this and
most other countries up to comparatively recent times. But it
was equally towards the end of his life that he made the assertion in the Seventh Letter, already quoted, to the effect that
philosophical truth could only be grasped by each individual
for himself after prolonged argument and discussion.

That does not, of course, mean that he pictured his ideal
society in the *Republic* as the scene of wide differences of

opinion, at any rate on fundamental issues. His attitude was, probably, rather like that of the Victorian scientists who believed that within measurable time all major problems would be solved by the application of the methods of science. For the matter of that, even the more modest scientists of our own day believe that some problems can be so solved. And when they have been solved the solution does not have to be enforced by law. For all those with the necessary ability and training can see for themselves that it is true, while the great mass of people accept the verdict of the scientists without question. That is the real modern parallel to the position that Plato assigns to his guardians. And it ought to make it clear that there is no real contradiction, such as superficial critics have tried to discover, between the freedom of discussion which Plato advocated and, so far as we know, encouraged in practice, and his notion of unity of opinion as an ideal.

The stimulus to our own thinking in all this is obvious. We should probably begin by asking ourselves whether Plato was justified in thinking that moral and political questions could ever become a matter of scientific demonstration. If not, is that due to the present imperfections of our knowledge, or is it an impossibility in principle which could never be overcome? To make clear to ourselves exactly where we should disagree with Plato on this point would be a fruitful exercise in thinking. And even when we have done this, a more general challenge remains. Those who, like John Stuart Mill, defend freedom of opinion and discussion as a necessary means of arriving at the truth, seem to imply by this argument that there is some prospect of arriving at the truth by those means. And they have to face the question what place remains for difference of opinion when the truth has been reached. That is putting in simple terms a very complicated question to which no short and easy answer is possible. But an examination of Plato's position is, at least, one very good way of starting us thinking about it.

There are many other points of which the same could be said. But the argument has already gone on too long. Where we should probably find least inspiration from Plato's thought would be in the problems, which occupy so much of our attention at the present time, of international relations and of duties of the individual outside the bounds of his own community. Plato's tendencies here were rather in the direction of what we should nowadays call isolationism, the exclusive concentration of the interests of the individual on his own community, which should be as self-sufficient as possible. In this he was developing to a logical conclusion the ordinary assumptions of orthodox Greek opinion in his time. There were, of course, certain tendencies in Greek thought which challenged the exclusive claim of his city on the individual, but they did not amount to anything serious till a generation or so after Plato's time, when political conditions had entirely changed. And when they did, they had to throw over a great deal that we should agree with Plato in thinking of value. If, for instance, we feel inclined, as some writers have done, to praise, by comparison with Plato, the amiable cosmopolitanism of Epicurus, we have to remember that that was the reverse side of his political quietism and renunciation of all public responsibilities. We do not, in fact, find anywhere in Greek thought very much help in arriving at that synthesis of patriotism and cosmopolitanism, of the need for which we are conscious, but which we are certainly very far from having found.

With this our task of conveying to the reader the main ideas of Plato's philosophy must end. Plato himself would probably have been the first to remind us that the study of any philosopher must, in the long run, be justified by the help it gives us in arriving at our own views. But the determined effort to see things as they presented themselves to him is in itself a valuable exercise for that purpose. And certainly, if we are going to make a study of a particular philosopher, it is worth while taking some trouble to ensure that it should be done with the greatest degree possible of fairness, sympathy, and understanding.

Appendix

FIELD'S BOOK is an admirable introduction to Plato's philosophy. Nevertheless, since it was first published in 1949 things have not stood still. For one, the study of Plato has continued as intensively as ever, and much new work has been published. Again, in philosophy generally there has been a marked in-interest in logical problems, in the use of the methods of logical analysis, and in the problems that arise from language and the ways in which language works. As the reader will note from pp. 146–7, Field was brought up in a rather different philosophical atmosphere, one which was more kindly to constructive metaphysics (he refers on p. 145 to Alexander and Whitehead as 'two of the most distinguished constructive metaphysicians of our time'), and less analytical than it has been in recent years. His tendency, then, is to present Plato rather from the side of traditional metaphysics and not to bring him into relation with more recent philosophy. Again much of Plato's political and social theory was under severe attack at the time when Field was writing, and here again he tended to rally to the traditional favourable interpretation. Now that, to some extent anyhow, the dust of battle has settled, it is perhaps possible to have a clearer and less committed view of the debate. The purpose of the notes that follow is to inform the reader of some of the more recent work on Plato, to alert him to some facets of Plato's philosophy which have particularly interested philosophers recently but are less prominent in Field's presentation, and to suggest some points that can perhaps now be seen in better perspective. They are mainly concerned with the theory of Forms (Chs. 2 and 3 of Field, with some references also to later chapters) and with Plato's political and social theory (primarily Chs. 4, 5, and the latter part of Ch. 10).

Field represents the theory of Forms as a metaphysical theory, an attempt (p. 17) to answer the question 'What is real?' —the Forms alone are completely real, the objects of the sensible world are only semi-real. With this he connects the role of the Forms in morals—they are the ideal standards which (p. 28) provide 'the basis of objective reality in our moral judgements'. Now these are two very important aspects of the theory of Forms, and Field sets them out with great clarity and force. On the other hand he has less to say (though he does say a certain amount in Ch. 3, Sec. 1, on pp. 33 ff.) about another aspect of the theory, where Plato is making an important contribution to logic, one which has been prominent and important in recent writing. This is the aspect where the Forms function as what in modern philosophy would be called universals. A discussion of the theory of Forms, including this aspect, will be found in R. C. Cross and A. D. Woozley, *Plato's Republic, A Philosophical Commentary* (1964), in Ch. 8, pp. 178 ff. To put the point briefly here, the problem is, in Field's words on p. 33, 'how a number of different things could also be one, as was implied by calling them all by the same name'. Plato's answer is that things in the world fall into groups in so far as the individual members of the group share in a single Form— the Form is the one over the many—and it is in virtue of this single Form, in which each of the members of the group share, that we are able to call them all by the same name. In more modern terms, the Form functions as a universal which may have many instances; and on the side of language, when we call each of a group of particulars by the same name, i.e. when we use a general term, the general term refers to the one Form or universal, in which all the members of the group share. Forms then account for our use of general terms, and of course most of the words in our language are general terms, used of many instances—for example 'man' is a general term, used of this man, that man, and so on; so 'white' of this white patch, that white patch; so 'is running' of this instance of running, that instance of running. Hence Plato, in the passage of the *Republic* (596a) to which Field is referring on p. 34, says, 'Shall we proceed as usual and begin by assuming the existence of a single essential nature or Form for every set of things which we call by the same name?' Hence, too, W. D. Ross (*Plato's Theory of Ideas* (1951), p. 225) writes: 'The essence of the theory of Ideas lay in the conscious recognition of the fact that there is a class of entities, for which the best name is probably "universals", that are entirely different from sensible things. Any use of language involves the recognition, either conscious or unconscious, of the fact that there are such entities; for every word used, except proper names—every abstract noun, every general noun, every adjective, every verb, even every pronoun and every preposition—is a name for something of which there are or may be instances.' For Ross, then, this is 'the essence of the theory of Ideas', whereas in Field, despite the discussion in Ch. 3, this logical strand in the theory is overshadowed by the prominence he gives to the purely metaphysical and to the moral aspects. It is important, however, for a number of reasons, that the reader should be fully aware of this logical element in the theory, however wrapped up it may be in metaphysical language. For one thing it is an element that does indubitably occur in Plato's own thinking; for another, it is a significant contribution to the logical problem of universals (a useful discussion of the problem, including Plato's contribution, will be found in A. D. Woozley, *Theory of Knowledge, An Introduction* (1949), Ch. iv); and again, it has a bearing on one's general interpretation of the theory of Forms and of the view one takes of Plato's own philosophical development. On this a little more must now be said.

First let us consider the question of what things Plato supposes there are Forms, i.e. the question of the range of the Forms. Now it is quite clear, as the reader will have gathered from Field, that in many of the dialogues it is Forms of mathematical objects and of moral qualities that interest Plato. On the other hand, if we consider what was said in the preceding paragraph, the range of the Forms would go far beyond these —there would, as Plato says in the *Republic* passage to which we referred, be a Form wherever there was a common name, i.e. a general term. Field, because he tends to write down the logical side of the theory, has similarly to write down this passage—'it is hard to believe', he says on p. 34, 'that he [Plato] meant that quite literally.' Again, on p. 34 he refers to the early part of the *Parmenides* (130b–130e), where Parmenides raises with Socrates this question of the range of the Forms. In this passage Socrates is quite clear about mathematical and moral Forms, is puzzled about Forms of man, fire, and water, and is very hesitant over Forms of trivial objects like hair, mud, or dirt. Field says that the general impression is that Plato, while not having reached a final decision, was inclined to postulate only moral and mathematical Forms. Parmenides' exhortation in 130e, however, at the end of the passage, that Socrates should not despise such objects (i.e. hair, mud, etc.) might lead one to the opposite impression, namely that the range of the Forms should be extended to cover all these cases, and this is the moral Ross draws in *Plato's Theory of Ideas* (p. 85). Indeed, the mere fact that in the dialogue the question of the range of the Forms is raised at all is significant, since it suggests that Plato saw that in principle his theory on its logical side extended beyond the specially favoured mathematical and moral Forms. Field returns to the question in Ch. 7, pp. 100–1. He thinks that Plato in the latest stage of his thought had abandoned the simple view of the *Republic* that there was a Form for each group of particulars to which we give a common name. In particular, he thinks from certain Aristotelian evidence that Plato would now deny Forms of manufactured objects such as, e.g., the Form of bed in the *Republic* (Bk. X, 596b). With this the reader should compare Ch. XI of Ross's book referred to above, which he entitles 'The Population of the World of Forms'. Ross convincingly interprets the Aristotelian evidence in such a way that it need not be taken as denying Forms of the products of the useful arts, and he reaches the conclusion (p. 175) that 'there is no real evidence that there was a later theory of Ideas in which Plato denied the existence of Ideas which he had earlier recognized'. Even granted this, however, the reader will see that there is an uneasiness within the theory of Forms. On the one hand, on the *Republic* principle the range of the Forms should be coextensive with our use of general terms;

on the other, the theory is concerned with the nature of reality and with moral standards, and the latter concerns may not be compatible with, or at any rate may raise problems in relation to, the more purely logical strand in the theory. This point about inner conflicts within the theory and the bearing this has on Plato's own development has been the subject of a good deal of attention in recent writing, and to this we now turn.

Field ends Ch. 2 with the remark that the general characteristics of the theory of Forms as he has described it 'continue to characterize it up to the last stage of Plato's thought'. The implication is that Plato continued to hold the theory without substantial modification throughout his life; and in a more general way the reader may gain the impression that the theory of Forms continues to be central in Plato's thought throughout. This view has come under scrutiny in recent writings. Before discussing it, however, we must refer to the Chronological Table on p. 165. In it the *Timaeus* is placed among the latest of Plato's dialogues, and this is the orthodox view about the dating of this dialogue. G. E. L. Owen, however ('The Place of the *Timaeus* in Plato's Dialogues' (1953), in *Studies in Plato's Metaphysics*, ed. R. E. Allen) and G. Ryle (*Plato's Progress* (1966), pp. 233 ff.) have argued that the *Timaeus* was written much earlier—around the time of the *Republic*, Owen suggests, and before the *Parmenides* and *Theaetetus*. Now the importance of this is that the theory of Forms appears in the *Timaeus* in the version familiar from the *Phaedo* and the *Republic*. Thus if the *Timaeus* is accepted as one of Plato's last dialogues, this seems strong evidence for the view represented by Field that Plato continued to hold the theory without substantial modification throughout his life. On the other hand, an earlier dating of the *Timaeus* would remove one obstacle at least from the way of those who wished to take a different view. Leaving aside now the specific question of the *Timaeus,* let us look at some of the considerations that have led to the questioning of the view that the theory of Forms, substantially unaltered, remains central to Plato's thought throughout his philosophical life. Much of this writing is contained in the essays collected by R. E. Allen in *Studies in Plato's Metaphysics* (1965), and Professor Allen explains the situation admirably in his Introduction (p. ix).

'There is', he says, 'a general issue which runs through many of the articles which follow, and which may well bear remark. It has to do with the question of whether Plato abandoned or sharply modified the Theory of Forms in later life; or if he did not, whether he consigned it to the back of his philosophical lumber-room, an outworn piece of machinery whose workings his developing and increasingly sophisticated interests had rendered largely obsolete.' To this issue the first part of the *Parmenides* (130a–135e) is crucial. There Plato puts into the mouth of Parmenides a series of criticisms of the theory of Forms, notably the criticism, which came to be known as the 'Third Man' argument,[1] that the theory involves an infinite regress; and he does not answer the criticisms. Two questions thus arise: first, are the criticisms damaging to the theory of Forms? and second, if they are, did Plato recognize this to be so? Field's view, which many other scholars have shared, is (p. 81) that the criticisms do not in fact deserve to be taken seriously—they are in the main purely verbal—and Plato neither took them very seriously nor modified his theories to meet them. This view has been questioned in more recent writing. In particular, in 1954 G. Vlastos published a paper, 'The Third Man Argument in the *Parmenides*' (reprinted in Professor Allen's book), in which he subjects the arguments in the *Parmenides* against the Forms to an extremely careful logical analysis, seeks to show the tacit premisses on which they depended, and argues that these premisses do in fact follow from the theory of Forms and cannot be altered or abandoned without fundamental modifications in the theory. His conclusions are the opposite of those of Field: the criticisms are valid, and, so far as Plato himself is concerned, the discussion in the *Parmenides* is, to use Vlastos's own words, 'the record of honest perplexity'—by the

---

[1] The 'Third Man' appears to have been a name given in antiquity to several different arguments directed against the existence of Forms. The one used in the *Parmenides* is of the following type: If 'man' is predicated of each of the particulars a, b, c, in virtue of their participation in the Form Man, the latter having an independent existence of its own, another Form (A Third Man) will be required, in virtue of which 'man' is predicated of the particulars a, b, c, and the Form Man. Similarly, a still further Form Man will be required in virtue of which 'man' is predicated of the particulars, the first Form, and the second, and so on, in an infinite regress.

time he came to write the *Parmenides* Plato is aware that something is wrong in the theory of Forms, but he is unable to put his finger on where the trouble lies. Vlastos's paper is an important one, and has given rise to much discussion which is not only important in relation to Plato, but philosophically fruitful in itself. Some of it will be found in other essays in Professor Allen's volume, and also in the *Proceedings of the Aristotelian Society* (Supplementary Volume XXXVII, 1963). The import of the first part of the *Parmenides* is then, at the least, an open question, and this in turn has its bearing on the role of the Forms in Plato's subsequent philosophical thinking. What is certainly true, and may not, perhaps, be sufficiently clear to the reader of Field's book, is that in the dialogues following the *Parmenides* (leaving aside the special case of the *Timaeus,* discussed earlier) Plato's interest shifts from the problems which were uppermost in his mind in dialogues like the *Phaedo* and *Republic.* Thus I. M. Crombie, who in certain ways is fairly conservative in his approach to Plato, in his book *An Examination of Plato's Doctrines* (Vol. II (1963), p. 356) says : 'As we have seen, Plato never abandoned the theory of forms, but it seems that after a certain date (roughly that of the *Republic*) he ceased to find it expedient to direct his readers' attention continually to "the very thing which is so-and-so", or to urge the importance of "recognizing the existence" of such entities. Universal properties continue to command a great deal of his attention, but there are a good many things which can be said about universal properties besides the things peculiar to the theory of forms, and it is with some of these that the later dialogues deal.' The reader will find a certain amount about these later developments in Sect. 5 of Ch. 9 in Field's book, but he may not realize how interesting and important they are, particularly, as in the *Sophist,* in their contribution to problems in logic. He will find more about this in, for example, some of the essays in Professor Allen's book, especially the well-known essay 'Plato's *Parmenides*' by G. Ryle (which includes comments also on the *Theaetetus* and *Sophist*), or again in Mr. Crombie's book referred to above (Vol. II, Part 3, Chs. ii ff., and Part 4), or in W. G. Runciman, *Plato's Later Epistemology* (1962).

It is time to turn now briefly to Field's account of Plato's political and social theory. When Field was writing his book Plato had for some time been under attack. For example, in 1934 Warner Fite, in *The Platonic Legend,* was severely critical of many of Plato's views, so again was R. H. S. Crossman, in *Plato Today*, published in 1939, and particularly so K. R. Popper, in *The Open Society and its Enemies,* Vol. I, first published in 1945. (Field probably has Popper amongst others in mind in Ch. 10, e.g. on pp. 147–8, though he is not mentioned by name in the text or in Field's own Bibliography.) Popper's book is a passionate book, possibly at various points wrong-headed and mistaken, but it is a book that anyone interested in political theory cannot afford not to read. Some of his main conclusions are that Plato regarded social change as degeneration, that his ideal state was designed to arrest social and political change, that it was thus a 'closed society', tribalistic and totalitarian in character; and with this he contrasts the 'open society', a society in which free individuals by their personal and responsible decisions can initiate change and build the kind of society they want. It will be clear to the reader that Field regards this sort of interpretation as a complete misrepresentation, and it could perhaps be, when one looks at the matter in perspective, that he reacts too far the other way in defence of Plato. At any rate, sometimes his analysis of Plato's argument could be pushed further with profit, and sometimes the significance of what Plato is saying tends to become blurred or to be given less importance than it seems to merit. Thus when Field is describing the evolution of the ideal city (pp. 51 ff.) he says rightly that Plato introduces the rulers under the principle of the division of labour. He does not, however, refer to the point, made convincingly by M. B. Foster in his penetrating analysis of Plato's arguments in Chs. i and ii of his book *The Political Philosophies of Plato and Hegel* (published in 1935), that the ideal city differs fundamentally from the 'first' city with which Plato began. The latter is an economic society based on the principle of the division of labour. The final 'ideal' city, whatever Plato says, is fundamentally different. It is a political society, and its tripartite division arises from something entirely different from the principle of the division of labour. To see this is to see something important for political theory, and it has a bearing on any discussion, as on pp. 152 ff., of the merits of Plato's proposals. Again, in case the reader should too easily accept Field's possibly over-favourable interpretation of Plato on certain points, attention may be called, for example, to p. 53 ('*La carrière ouverte aux talents* is a fundamental principle of the *Republic*'), pp. 59–61 (consent and freedom in the ideal state), pp. 72–3 (the happiness of the city and the happiness of the individuals in it), pp. 129 ff. (Plato on the use of deception—in addition to the Foundation Myth, which Field discusses, the reader should also look at *Republic* 459–60, where the deception to be practised by the rulers in arranging marriages is described), and p. 131 (the suggestion of a common basic education). In these, and other places too, the reader is urged to look carefully at the text of Plato, and weigh the significance of what Plato is saying. In this he may find useful the references and discussion in Chs. 4 and 5 of Cross and Woozley, *Plato's Republic, A Philosophical Commentary*, referred to earlier. Lastly, the reader's attention may be called to a very exhaustive study, *In Defense of Plato*, by R. B. Levinson, published in 1953, in which Professor Levinson (p. 25, footnote) refers to 'Field's defense of Plato' in Ch. 10 of the present work. Levinson's aim is to examine in great detail what Plato's critics, especially Popper, have to say, and to seek to answer them. His book is useful particularly for the detailed references to the text of Plato that it gives, and of which the reader may feel the lack in *The Philosophy of Plato*.

R. C. Cross

Note on Chronology

THE READER must be warned that, though the order of the main groups of the dialogues can be established with a fair degree of probability, the actual dates assigned to particular dialogues, except in one or two instances, are highly conjectural. The grounds, such as they are, for the conjectures can be found in my *Plato and his Contemporaries*.

B.C.		
427	Plato's birth.	
399	Death of Socrates.	
		Ion, Apology, Crito and other lesser dialogues.
		Protagoras.
		Lysis. Charmides.
392		*Gorgias.*
		Meno.
387 (about)	First visit to Sicily.	
		Cratylus.
385 (about)	Foundation of the Academy.	*Phaedo.*
383		*Symposium.*
375 to 368		*Republic.*
		Phaedrus.
		Parmenides.
		Theaetetus.
367	Second visit to Sicily.	
362	Third visit to Sicily.	
		Sophist.
		Politicus.
		Philebus.
		Timaeus.
		Laws and *Epinomis*.
347	Plato's death.	

Bibliography

THE ORIGINAL Bibliography was prefaced by the following note:

There is a vast literature on Plato in all languages. It is only possible here to present a selection of works which seem likely to be of the most service to an English reader. The list has been confined to work which has appeared in book form, and no attempt has been made to catalogue all the various studies of particular points which are to be found scattered throughout the learned periodicals, though these have often made most valuable contributions to the understanding of Plato.

The same general principles have been followed in this revision.

(a) *TEXT of all the dialogues*:

Ed. by J. Burnet (Oxford Classical Texts, Oxford, Clarendon Press). With an English Translation, by various hands (Loeb Classical Library, London, Heinemann; Cambridge, Mass., Harvard University Press). With a French Translation, by various hands (Budé, Les Belles Lettres, Paris).

(b) *TRANSLATION of all the dialogues*:

The Dialogues of Plato, with Analyses and Introductions, by B. Jowett, 4th edn., revised (Oxford, Clarendon Press, 1953). See also (a) above (Loeb Classical Library).

(c) *EDITIONS, TRANSLATIONS, and COMMENTARIES on particular dialogues*:

    (i) TEXT, INTRODUCTION, and NOTES:

    Euthyphro, Apology, Crito, by J. Burnet (Oxford, Clarendon Press, 1924).
    Gorgias, by E. R. Dodds (Oxford, Clarendon Press, 1959).

Meno, by R. S. Bluck (Cambridge, C.U.P., 1961).

Phaedo, by J. Burnet (Oxford, Clarendon Press, 1911).

Republic, by J. Adam, 2nd edn., ed. by D. A. Rees (Cambridge, C.U.P., 1963).

Timaeus, with a Translation, by R. D. Archer-Hind (London, Macmillan, 1888).

Theaetetus, by L. Campbell (Oxford, Clarendon Press, 1883).

Sophist and *Politicus*, by L. Campbell (Oxford, Clarendon Press, 1867).

Philebus, by R. G. Bury (Cambridge, C.U.P., 1897).

Seventh and Eighth Letters, by R. S. Bluck (Cambridge, C.U.P., 1947).

(ii) TRANSLATIONS, with INTRODUCTION and NOTES of varying length:

Euthyphro, Apology, Crito, Phaedo, Gorgias, by W. D. Woodhead (Edinburgh, Nelson, 1953).

Republic, by A. D. Lindsay, revised edn. (Everyman Library, London, Dent, 1920).

Republic, by F. M. Cornford (Oxford, Clarendon Press, 1941).

Republic, by H. D. P. Lee (London, Penguin Books, 1955).

Timaeus and *Critias*, by A. E. Taylor (London, Methuen, 1929).

Phaedrus, Lysis, Protagoras, by J. Wright (London, Macmillan, 1900).

Parmenides, by A. E. Taylor (Oxford, Clarendon Press, 1934).

Symposium, by W. Hamilton (London, Penguin Books, 1951).

Sophist and *Politicus*, by A. E. Taylor (Edinburgh, Nelson, 1961).

Politicus, by J. B. Skemp (London, Routledge, 1952).

Philebus and *Epinomis*, by A. E. Taylor (Edinburgh, Nelson, 1956).

Laws, by A. E. Taylor (Everyman Library, London, Dent, 1934; New York, Dutton, 1961).

Letters, by L. A. Post (Oxford, Clarendon Press, 1925).

Letters, by G. R. Morrow (Illinois Studies in Language and Literature, XVIII, 1935).

(iii) TRANSLATIONS with full running COMMENTARY (the Greekless reader will find these particularly useful):

Phaedo, by R. S. Bluck (London, Routledge, 1955; New York, Bobbs Merrill, 1959).

Phaedo, by R. Hackforth (Cambridge, C.U.P., 1955).

Plato's Cosmology (Timaeus), by F. M. Cornford (London, Routledge, 1937; paperback, New York, Bobbs Merrill, 1957).

Phaedrus, by R. Hackforth (Cambridge, C.U.P., 1952; New York, Bobbs Merrill, 1952).

Plato and Parmenides, by F. M. Cornford (London, Routledge, 1939; paperback, New York, Bobbs Merrill, 1957).

Plato's Theory of Knowledge (*Theaetetus* and *Sophist*), by F. M. Cornford (London, Routledge, 1935; New York, Humanities, 1965).

Plato's Examination of Pleasure (*Philebus*), by R. Hackforth (Cambridge, C.U.P., 1945).

(iv) COMMENTARY only:

Plato's 'Republic', *A Philosophical Commentary*, by R. C. Cross and A. D. Woozley (London, Macmillan, 1964; New York, St. Martins, 1964).

A Commentary on Plato's 'Timaeus', by A. E. Taylor (Oxford, Clarendon Press, 1928).

(d) *GENERAL WORKS:*

Allen, R. E. (ed.), *Studies in Plato's Metaphysics* (London, Routledge, 1965; New York, Humanities, 1965).

Bambrough, R. (ed.), *Plato, Popper and Politics* (Cambridge, Heffer, 1967; New York, Barnes & Noble, 1967).

Barker, E., *Greek Political Theory: Plato and his Predecessors* (London, Methuen, 1918); revised edn. (cloth and paperback, New York, Barnes & Noble, 1947).

Burnet, J., *Greek Philosophy from Thales to Plato* (London, Macmillan, 1914, paperback 1961; New York, St. Martins, 1914).

Crombie, I. M., *An Examination of Plato's Doctrines* (London, Routledge, vol. i 1962, vol. ii 1963; New York, Humanities, i 1962, ii 1963).

Crombie, I. M., *Plato, the Midwife's Apprentice* (London, Routledge, 1964; New York, Barnes & Noble, 1965).

Field, G. C., *Plato and his Contemporaries*, 2nd edn. (London, Methuen, 1948, paperback 1967).

Foster, M. B., *The Political Philosophies of Plato and Hegel* (Oxford, Clarendon Press, 1935).

Gould, J., *The Development of Plato's Ethics* (Cambridge, C.U.P., 1955).

Grube, G. M. A., *Plato's Thought* (London, Methuen, 1935; paperback, New York, Beacon, 1958).

Jaeger, W., *Paideia*, 2nd edn. (Oxford, Blackwell, 1944, 1945; New York, O.U.P., 1945).

Levinson, R. B., *In Defense of Plato* (Cambridge, Mass., Harvard University Press, 1953).

Popper, K. R., *The Open Society and its Enemies*, 4th edn. (cloth and paperback, London, Routledge, 1962).

Robin, L., *Greek Thought* (London, Kegan Paul, 1928; New York, Russell & Russell, 1967).

Ross, W. D., *Plato's Theory of Ideas* (Oxford, Clarendon Press, 1951).

Runciman, W. G., *Plato's Later Epistemology* (Cambridge, C.U.P., 1962).

Ryle, G., *Plato's Progress* (Cambridge, C.U.P., 1966).

Shorey, P., *What Plato Said* (Chicago, University of Chicago Press, 1933).

Solmsen, F., *Plato's Theology* (Ithaca, Cornell University Press, 1942).

Taylor, A. E., *Plato: The Man and his Work,* 7th edn. (cloth and paper-back, London, Methuen, 1960; New York, Barnes & Noble, 1961).

Wedberg, A., *Plato's Philosophy of Mathematics* (Stockholm, Almquist & Wiksell, 1955).

Woozley, A. D., *Theory of Knowledge. An Introduction* (London, Hutchinson, 1949, paperback 1966).

R. C. Cross

Index